The Human Side of Reference and Information Services in Academic Libraries

CHANDOS
INFORMATION PROFESSIONAL SERIES

Series Editor: Ruth Rikowski
(email: Rikowskigr@aol.com)

Chandos' new series of books are aimed at the busy information professional. They have been specially commissioned to provide the reader with an authoritative view of current thinking. They are designed to provide easy-to-read and (most importantly) practical coverage of topics that are of interest to librarians and other information professionals. If you would like a full listing of current and forthcoming titles, please visit our web site **www.chandospublishing.com** or contact Hannah Grace-Williams on email info@chandospublishing.com or telephone number +44 (0) 1865 884447.

New authors: we are always pleased to receive ideas for new titles; if you would like to write a book for Chandos, please contact Dr Glyn Jones on email gjones@chandospublishing.com or telephone number +44 (0) 1865 884447.

Bulk orders: some organisations buy a number of copies of our books. If you are interested in doing this, we would be pleased to discuss a discount. Please contact Hannah Grace-Williams on email info@chandospublishing.com or telephone number +44 (0) 1865 884447.

The Human Side of Reference and Information Services in Academic Libraries

Adding value in the digital world

EDITED BY LESLEY S. J. FARMER

Chandos Publishing
Oxford · England

Chandos Publishing (Oxford) Limited
Chandos House
5 & 6 Steadys Lane
Stanton Harcourt
Oxford OX29 5RL
UK
Tel: +44 (0) 1865 884447 Fax: +44 (0) 1865 884448
Email: info@chandospublishing.com
www.chandospublishing.com

First published in Great Britain in 2007

ISBN
978 1 84334 257 1 (paperback)
978 1 84334 258 8 (hardback)
1 84334 257 X (paperback)
1 84334 258 8 (hardback)

© The contributors, 2007

Typeset by Avocet Typeset, Chilton, Aylesbury, Bucks.
Printed and bound in the UK by 4edge Ltd, Hockley. www.4edge.co.uk

Dedicated to
The Library Staff at
California State University, Long Beach

Contents

Preface

Higher education serves as the intellectual vanguard for civilisation. In this environment, knowledge is created, discussed, and disseminated in the service of society. Academic freedom posits that these intellectual processes will be unfettered by political or other socio-economic agendas. The ultimate goal is *truth*.

The academic universe, it should be noted, is not a closed one. One of the aims of universities is to pass on knowledge to future generations. Nowadays, it would be more accurate to say that faculty and students share their experiences and perspectives, and engage together in knowledge discernment and development, supported by their respective learning communities.

Additionally, academia has a social responsibility to pursue knowledge for the good of the whole, to improve the world. Publicly-funded institutions, in particular, need to respond to the needs and demands of the greater population.

In short, responsible and responsive information is at the heart of the university.

The library's role

Where do reference librarians fit into this picture, especially in the digital age? Some might say nowhere. Reference librarians, in particular, serve as mediators between information seekers and the information itself. If the librarian *impedes* the connection, then a disservice has been done. If, however, the librarian *facilitates* that connection, then a value-added service has occurred.

Within the academic world, the library plays a central role as its staff collects, organises, stores, preserves, and exchanges information. As the academic community conducts research, it needs to review the existing literature, and so depends on the library's resources and networks to the world of information. Timely and convenient access to relevant information has never been so important.

Likewise, as students learn how to locate, understand and apply existing knowledge, they need to develop their information competence. As expert information processors, librarians can help them access information intellectually directly and through collaboration with teaching faculty. Librarians can also help the rest of the academic community to hone their information skills.

Librarian participation on campus committees can optimise data-driven decision-making and facilitate institutional improvement as they research campus issues and communicate findings. Their input on policies fosters the habit of lifelong learning.

Librarians also need to keep current in their own field, accessing a rich collection of resources and experts to develop their own professional competence and promote knowledge with their professional peers.

Combining campus contributions, a significant campus-wide value-added reference/information service is a knowledge management service whereby institutional documents are contributed to a central repository to be indexed and made available to the academic community for data harvesting. Such a service requires the voluntary participation of stakeholders.

The impact of technology on information and reference services

Academic librarians have embraced technology from the start: handwritten to typeset books, typewriters to Library of Congress cards, CD-ROM subscription databases to online versions. Reference librarians have expanded John Cotton Dana's quote: 'the right book to the right person at the right time' to incorporate the phrase 'in the right format'.

As the academic community – including incoming students – experience technology in their daily lives, they expect technology when they enter the library doors. Even those individuals who are not comfortable with technology expect the kind of reference service that now requires the incorporation of technology: access to journals and books, answers to academic questions, techniques for research strategies. The academic community usually is not interested in the searching process per se; they just want to find the answers. Their ideal reference experience is a one-stop searching process that integrates different formats and sources seamlessly, using each person's natural vocabulary and schema ('folksonomies').

In response, reference librarians have to decide what technology will enhance – or otherwise influence their services. In some cases, they can choose to pursue a technological solution, such as 24/7 reference service. In other cases, technology is thrust upon them, such as integrated library systems or online subscription databases. (True, academic libraries *could* stick with manual circulation systems, but the time saved in records management is worth getting the automated system.) Particularly as more journals and indexes are transitioning to electronic form only, reference librarians need to make sure that these scholarly tools are made available to their constituents. Frankly, while service should drive technology decisions, in actuality the two entities have a symbiotic relationship; awareness of a new technology solution or product can, for example, open up new service options.

In any case, technology for today's reference service constitutes more than a simple expansion of purchasing another laptop. It requires sufficient front-end and sustainable funding, effective management, and a fully articulated technology system that interfaces with the entire campus, and links to other library service networks. Whatever the technology solution, it should be reliable and stable – fitting the library's resources and services.

The human side of technology for reference services

All the technology in the world will not ensure high-quality academic reference services without an equally high-quality human deployment. No longer can one person be expected to take care of all things technological. Moreover, administrative decision-makers, such as library deans, have to recognise their limitations in the area of technology, and use their personnel savvy to hire technologists with the skill sets needed to implement the library's technology plan. In order to ensure success in incorporating technology into reference services, library deans need to apply their management skills and influence to coordinate the overall service plan, integrating the technology aspect as seamlessly as possible. Furthermore, technology experts need to work together: among themselves, with non-technical library staff, and with the rest of the academic community. Tacit knowledge needs to be shared explicitly and clearly so that the entire enterprise can act on the information. Not only do people need to share and learn a variety of specialist vocabularies and acronyms (e.g. LC, ILL, CSS, VoIP, RFID, PHP), but they also need to observe and translate user needs into appropriate resources and services. Indeed, all library functions start with their clientele – a traditional value that holds equally well in the digital age.

Interdependence of campus technology and library reference services

Just as the library's function supports the entire academic community, technology-enhanced library reference functions are likely to interface with other parts of the campus.

- *Electronic reserves.* This manual task can be hard for teaching faculty to use and labour-intensive for library staff. An e-reserve software program provides a user-friendly interface for 'ordering' and retrieving reserved materials. With technology, these faculty members can build a bibliography rather than bringing documents to the library for processing and circulating. Many sources can be located in electronic form and digitised (and compressed). With a central repository and database, documents can be linked to several courses simultaneously, and tracked to ensure copyright compliance. The Aires electronic reserve program, which incorporates copyright management, can also be integrated into online learning management systems.

- *Electronic delivery.* Increasingly, documents are available in digital form, facilitating their delivery to requesters. In addition, the use of fax/scanners linked to Internet-connected computers enables print documents to be transferred electronically. These procedures have several benefits: quicker turn-around time, less labour, cheaper transfer/mailing costs, greater access to the information, cost-effective resource sharing, and less wear-and-tear on the original document. Prospero from Ohio State University is a freeware program that manages electronic document service delivery effectively.

- *Distance instruction.* Increasingly, campuses provide videotaping services and studios to produce professional-quality results. Library lectures can be videotaped, edited, rendered and streamed through the library's portal in order to optimise instructional outreach. With technical help, video content can also be assembled into an interactive tutorial and stored either on a server or duplicated onto optical disc for user convenience. Especially as more campuses serve distance learners, real-time video-enhanced instruction offers a way to ameliorate the disadvantages of off-campus connections. Cohort models, with groups of students clustered geographically, can take advantage of remote videoconferencing installations so that librarians can actually see and interact with these students 'live'.

- *Library automation systems.* Patron records can interface with campus registration records, facilitating patron information maintenance and tying overdue/lost fines to other fiscal responsibilities of the individual.

- *Library collection replacement management.* Circulation and interlibrary loan statistics can identify books that need replacement, interfacing with automated ordering and processing systems. This kind of integrated approach also keeps better track of document status and budgets.

- *Lecture requests.* Using an SQL server, an online faculty request can interface with a library scheduling database, facilitating timely sign-ups and documenting service levels. As librarians become more proactive about delivering information literacy instruction, they may need to go to other campus computer labs, thus necessitating the need for a campus-wide lab scheduling program.

- *24/7 online reference service.* As students want reference help anytime from anywhere, online reference service has become a necessity service, even if the only method is e-mail. To accommodate the 3 a.m. researcher, libraries are entering into online reference service consortia with other academics around the world or with other types of library systems across borders. In the process, librarians from each campus may well be serving members of other institutions. Not only does this practice impact Internet activity, but the issues of authentification and security firewalls are notched up a level as campus technology services have to figure out how to provide safe, ongoing access. On a administrative level, librarians need to make sure that policies are established that support such intra-campus agreements. Likewise, other campus technology-related services can be improved if they know about library reference services. Librarians need to identify other campus resources and services, and communicate with them about library technology in order to optimise both operations.

- *Faculty instructional design and development centres*. Designers tend to focus on course management systems. In the process, they have the potential to mention library technology resources and show how to interface with those sources and services.

- *Audio-visual centres*. Many campuses offer a central office to circulate audio-visual equipment, such as data projectors and laptop computers. If the library provides wi-fi access, then those circulating systems might need to have wi-fi cards installed in them.

- *Software licensing and distribution*. Increasingly, campuses adopt a suite of productivity application software programs for faculty use. With their experience in subscribing to online databases and inventorying resources, librarians can suggest procedures to the offices in charge of such procurements in order to streamline operations.

Value-added service

In the final analysis, academic librarians need to provide – and publicise – value-added information and reference service. Particularly in a Google age, individuals might not realise how much they are missing in terms of relevant and important information. While students and even faculty may settle for 'good enough' resources, their criteria for an adequate level of information may well be uninformed. Reference librarians need to show the academic community what resources are available – and how to access them effectively.

Even with technology-enhanced storage and retrieval tools, such a warehouse model of reference service is inadequate. Even the most traditional academic libraries provide ready reference service so clientele can get the answer they need, be it a fact or a process question. While librarians are well trained to be responsive to users' needs, with the advent of Ask.com and Yahoo's question/answer features, the academic community might well bypass the librarian as a source of information. How can the academic librarian serve as an effective mediator in the digital age?

Today's academic librarians need to assess the informational needs and wants of the academic community proactively, expanding reference services and developing information products to anticipate those identified demands. Traditional collection development has carried out this philosophy. These days, the ante has been raised to include products and services that apply technology. Some of the possibilities include:

- Subject webliographies
- localised databases of experts
- learning object repositories
- campus-wide knowledge management systems
- metasearching interfaces
- RSS feeds about research interests
- diagnostic-based information literacy web tutorials.

Resultant user-based references services can significantly affect the academic community – if they are well marketed and publicised. As with the other parts of the reference service process, telling the library's story can be facilitated through technology, but only if that technology is grounded in human endeavour. Thus, library blogs, podcasting, and connections made with existing course management systems use communication channels that resonate with the modern, 'Millennial' student.

Global perspectives

Understandably, reference and information services vary widely around the world, depending on library resources and librarian expertise, as well as the expectations of their academic communities and larger societies. For instance, in a society where information transfer maintains a stable culture, higher education access to largely uncontrollable information sources online is not a priority goal. In areas where electricity is at a premium, technology-based reference services are out of the question. Nevertheless, all academic librarians have the responsibility to support academic agendas.

Academic librarians in developing countries need to ascertain the needs of their clientele, and prioritise the technologies needed to carry out their mission. In some cases, the most important activity is to communicate with professional peers in order to identify possible reference solutions that integrate technology. In other cases, academic librarians need to focus on information literacy instruction.

In any case, the core features of reference services need to be examined on an international basis, and parsed in terms of technology requirements, personnel expertise and community connections. Professional organisations should offer guidance so that academic librarians can collaborate with their peers to provide twenty-first century information and reference services that integrate technology effectively.

Organisation of this book

This book was developed as a university library case study with global implications. Professional staff contributed to each chapter, providing a unique lens to the overall library information and reference service programme.

Consistent with the philosophy of library service, Chapter 1 examines the impact of technology on the information needs and behaviours of the academic community. Not only do the clientele reflect an increasingly diverse population, but their technology experiences further broaden the spectrum of needs and skills.

Chapter 2 explores technology's impact on reference and information services staffing. New skills sets and new approaches to service have created a fluid and challenging management issue.

Chapter 3 deals with reference resources. Traditionally a relatively stable endeavour, technology has introduced many more possibilities and challenges.

Although librarians have 'packaged' information for years, particularly in the form of bibliographies, the need and benefit of value-added manipulation of information has grown exponentially with the advent of technology. Chapter 4 deals with the changing role of the librarian in this regard.

Technology impacts the academic community's physical access to reference and information resources, as detailed in Chapter 5. Digital resources themselves raise issues of equipment and connectivity, and the varying physical demands of users, such as visual impairment, require library staff to re-examine their practices.

Just as important, is the influence of technology with respect to intellectual access to information and reference services. Both ready reference and instruction have changed, as a result. These issues are addressed in Chapter 6.

The final chapter examines the role of evaluation in optimising the human use of technology for academic reference services. Planning should incorporate assessment from the start so that librarians can tell if their mission is accomplished. Throughout the development and deployment of reference and information services, efforts need to be documented and assessed. As data are analysed, plans can be adjusted to improve service and its impact. Technological tools can facilitate this process, but the difference that the assessment makes depends on the insight, creativity and collaboration of the academic community.

A bibliography and index conclude the volume.

Do information and reference services matter in the digital age? Indeed! Academic library staff continue to serve as intellectual mediators in a world where information is rampant and sometimes disreputable. One key to the endurance of academic libraries is their humane application of resources, including technology, in support of serviceable knowledge for the good of society. As a small contribution in this arena, all proceeds of this book will be used to underwrite scholarships for individuals pursuing a library credential or degree at California State University, Long Beach.

About the contributors

Dr Lesley Farmer, Professor at California State University Long Beach, coordinates the Library Media Teacher programme. She earned her MS in Library Science at the University of North Carolina Chapel Hill, and received her doctorate in Adult Education from Temple University. Dr Farmer has worked as a professional librarian in academic, public, special and K-12 school settings. A frequent presenter and writer for the profession, Dr Farmer's most recent books include *Librarians, Literacy and the Promotion of Gender Equity* (McFarland, 2005) and *Digital Inclusion, Teens, and Your Library* (Libraries Unlimited, 2005). Her research interests include information literacy, collaboration and educational technology.

Joseph Aubele has served as a Reference & Instructional Librarian at California State University Long Beach since 2004. He received his MLIS degree from UCLA. He serves as the subject specialist librarian for criminal justice, economics, professional studies and psychology. His research interests include information literacy and information seeking behaviours.

Henry DuBois is Administrative Services Librarian at California State University Long Beach (CSULB). He earned his MLS at UC Berkeley and a Masters in Public Administration at CSULB. During his nearly 40 years with the library he has served as a department head for the humanities and fine arts reference departments, media resources librarian, collection development officer, and Associate Dean. He has been an elected officer, programme planner, and presenter for the ACRL Arts Section and for the LAMA Safety and Security of Libraries Committee. He currently serves on the EBSCO Publishing Academic Libraries Advisory Board.

Susan B. Jackson is Business Librarian at California State University Long Beach. She earned her MS in Library Science and her MA in

History at the University of Illinois, Urbana-Champaign. Ms Jackson has been a law librarian, government documents librarian as well as a business librarian. She enjoys working with students, and will be conducting research on their information-seeking behavior.

Tracey Mayfield is Associate Librarian at California State University Long Beach and the librarian subject specialist for family and consumer sciences, human development, recreation and leisure and kinesiology. She earned her BA in English and her MLIS from UCLA where she worked for the UCLA Libraries for ten years. Ms Mayfield has an extensive background in library building services, library services for the disabled, and is currently working on research about library services for older students, as well as the importance of mentoring new librarians and MLIS students through internships. Ms Mayfield is currently Southern Vice President/President-Elect of the California Academic and Research Libraries (CARL), the California chapter of ACRL.

Sara B. Sluss is the Interim Associate Dean of the California State University Long Beach Library and Academic Technology Services. She received a Master of Library Science from Emporia State University (Kansas) and Master of Science in Publishing from Pace University (New York City). Prior to her current appointment, she was content manager for the CSULB Library's websites and served as business librarian. Before moving to California in 1995, Ms Sluss served as the Associate Librarian for Reader Services at Baruch College Library/City University of New York.

Tiffini Travis is the Director of Information Literacy and Outreach Services at California State University Long Beach. She earned her BA in political science at UC Berkeley and her MLIS at UCLA. She recently joined ACRL's immersion programme faculty of nationally recognised librarians. Presenting both nationally and internationally, her research interests include information literacy assessment, student use of the Internet for research, and website usability.

The authors may be contacted care of the Editor:

E-mail: *lfarmer@csulb.edu*

Technology impact on information needs and behaviours of the academic community

Joseph Aubele, Susan Jackson and Lesley Farmer

An undergraduate student e-mails a reference librarian to get some help on a business communications class project. The topic is 'nonverbal communication in relation to management'. He writes that he is stuck and is unable to get any information on any relevant topics. The librarian replies, asking where he has looked for information. The librarian instructs the student to use the library's business databases, and the student replies that he found nothing useful on his topic in those databases. At this point, the librarian has no idea what keywords this student used or how many articles he found. This student has not been clear about his needs and had difficulty expressing what he is actually looking for. The librarian continues to help this student by conducting her own search on a database and examining the results of her search. At this point, she can direct the student to some relevant material on his topic, and give him some keywords and subjects to use to continue his research.

A new instructor from Bangkok remembers a seminal work available in her homeland, and wants to access it for her upcoming course. However, she is not familiar with some of the subscription databases available at her new university, which may be useful for her students. She is also nervous because her department is requiring her to mount class readings onto the campus course management system. The librarian explains that an orientation to the library and its resources, including online databases, can be provided for her and the class. In the meantime, though, the librarian shows the instructor how to use the library's online interlibrary loan request form to obtain the needed Thai document.

An undergraduate student visits the reference desk. He is taking an English course and needs some critical analysis on Ernest Hemingway. He has no idea where to begin his search for information. The librarian at the desk teaches the student how to use the library's online catalogue to find books on the author. She shows him the correct subject headings and where to find these books. She also encourages the student to return to her if he decides he wants additional information. The librarian wants to avoid overwhelming the student with too much information.

University libraries serve a wide spectrum of users. Most belong to the institution's academic community, but some are community members. If the library is a public institution, it probably has to serve those neighbourhood residents. The ever-present quandary is how academic librarians affect the academics who are present at instruction sessions, visit the reference desk, and contact subject librarians for research appointments. Who are these constituents? In a larger sense, how do these individuals behave, and what are they thinking about research and the research process? Academic reference librarians need to define these people so they can affect their information seeking behaviour. If academic librarians can understand them, then they can positively affect their search for information and give them the tools needed to evaluate the information they find.

The Millennials: a new species

The generation now called the Millennial Generation (a.k.a Generation Y, Echo Boom, Baby Boomlets, and Fourteenth Generation) is made up of young people born since the early 1980s. While most of the literature focuses on the experience of youth in the USA, the impact of technology and globalisation has shaped the lives of Millennials around the world. The annual Beloit College (Wisconsin) Mindset List (*http://www.beloit .edu/~pubaff/mindset*) provides valuable insights into the social and cultural experiences that have helped shape today's entering freshmen class. For instance, the class of 2010 think carbon copies are antique oddities, know that Disneyland has always been in Europe and Asia, and have always been able to 'watch wars and revolutions live on television'. At the same time, cultural and individual differences abound so that no one set of characteristics can definitively define this entire age group.

Nevertheless, some trends emerge that can inform academic librarians.

Howe and Strauss (2003) define Millennials as smart, ambitious, incredibly busy, very ethnically diverse, and dominated by girls. This Baby Boomlet population of 79 million are family-oriented, driven to success, viscerally pluralistic, deeply committed to authenticity and truth-telling, heavily stressed, and living in a no-boundaries world where they make short-term decisions and expect paradoxical outcomes (Leo, 2003).

'They are special, sheltered, confident, team-oriented, achieving, pressured, conventional and they have a special relationship to technology. They are not all tech-savvy but they have a special attachment to the power of the new technology tools' (Rainie, 2006: 3). For Millennials, the Web is a much more interpersonal experience than just browsing web pages. Millennials are heavy 'users of instant messaging and online chat'. Additionally, 95 per cent of those surveyed indicated that they use e-mail for 'social communication at least once a week' (Jones, 2002).

In Sax's 2003 analysis about incoming college freshmen for 2002, she explored a couple of additional trends: financing education, supporting gay rights, stress, and interest in the arts. In terms of political affiliation, 2002 signalled a shift back toward more moderate and conservative political orientation rather than the more liberal labels used in the previous five years. Students responded that they did not feel connected to politics, but believed they could have an effect on their communities, accomplishing this by getting involved in activities through schools, religious groups, and other service organisations. Other trends included support for legalising marijuana, contrasting with a decline in cigarette smoking and drinking; the anti-drug campaigns occurring in elementary and middle schools appear to have had an affect on students' behaviour.

In terms of academics, there seemed to be a paradox: the 2002 students had higher grades but were spending less time studying. In 2002, the percentage of students averaging 'A' grades in secondary school reached 45.7 per cent, compared with an all-time low of 17.6 per cent in 1968 (Sax, 2003: 16). In direct contrast, the percentage of students devoting six or more hours per week to studying or homework declined to an all-time low of 33.4 per cent in 2002, compared with a high of 47 per cent when this question was first asked on the 1987 survey. Sax suggested several factors that could have contributed to this situation: increased competition for college admission leading students to become more productive and better time managers, an increasing number of students taking secondary school advanced placement courses that boosted grade point averages, and more student self-confidence about attending college.

As students, Millennials are smart and expect immediate results. These students want to be able to makes choices and customise their choice; they want to learn what they need to know, and prefer to learn by doing. Technology natives, they carry all manner of electronic devices, particularly portable ones: PDAs, cell phones, laptops and MP3 players. They multi-task, instant messaging while surfing the Internet, listening to music, and doing their homework (Carlson, 2005). Ninety per cent of white male college students have gone online, compared with about 60 per cent of the general population; even black students, the lowest-using college subgroup, went online more (74 per cent) than their general population counterparts (45 per cent). About 42 per cent use the Internet to communicate socially, and 38 per cent use it for schoolwork (Jones, 2002). Surprisingly, Millennials are often unaware of and indifferent to the consequences of their use of technology (Rainie, 2006). These students are great at using communication devices, but their communication skills in terms of writing and speaking are not well-developed (Carlson, 2005).

These qualities of the Millennials can be observed in academic student bodies. Although technologically adept, they do not understand the research process. They know how to download music to their MP3 players, how to set up their laptops and download software. Most of them have cell phones, and are in constant touch with friends and family. They are a generation that played video games. Yet many Millenials do not understand that research takes time; they would prefer to sit down at a computer, type in a couple of words, and get a list of full-text articles that they can read. They do not always understand the thought process necessary for research. They want their information delivered quickly and easily and accessible from anywhere.

Examining the information processes of undergraduates, Holliday and Li (2004) noted how the nature of technology affected the students' cognitive processes. The ease of using Google to generate multiple sources of information on a topic, cutting-and-pasting from full-text articles online, and word processing a paper can shortcut reflective research habits. Once they find a possible 'hit', students often settle for 'good enough' information rather than critically comparing sources or refocusing their research questions and strategy. Students seem to be intellectually skimming.

An additional fear exists that higher education is catering to these 'too fast' students, that faculty are more concerned with students' feelings than desiring to teach them useful information. University linguistics professor Naomi Baron sees today's students as 'products not just of a constant information barrage, but also of an educational system that has lost its ability to impart skills' (Carlson, 2005: A36). It appears that universities and students are in collusion to focus on satisfaction rather than academic rigor.

Library experiences of Millennials

The vast majority of students at most colleges and universities come from the Millennial generation. While there is little doubt that libraries represent an invaluable component in the intellectual development of students, there is also a palpable sense among academic librarians that Millennials arrive ill-prepared, and in some cases, incapable of conducting even the most rudimentary scholarly research. Those looking for evidence of this view need not look any further than the ubiquity of the bibliographic instruction/information literacy sessions conducted in libraries, the vast majority of which focus on the research tools (e.g. online catalogue, research databases, etc.) that students might utilise. However, these sessions all but ignore the information seeking behaviours of this technologically-savvy demographic. Academic librarians do so at not only their own peril, but to the detriment of the students being served. Enhancing their own understanding of the information experiences of Millennials enables librarians to meet the needs and expectations of this constituent group more effectively, and in the process enhance their ability to conduct effective research as they visit the 'virtual' library as well as the actual library building (Duck and Koeske, 2005).

Academic librarians can apply Millennials' intensive and interpersonal use of technology to help them evaluate information. Rather than naïve acceptance of the Web and all it contains, Millennials appear to be more informationally sophisticated than some might realise. In fact, today's Millennial is more correctly described as an 'information player', defined by Nicholas (2003) as 'information seeking [that] can be interactive, recreational, social, competitive and acknowledges the characteristics of individuality and activity that define today's online engagements' (Nicholas, 2003: 23). Academic librarians can use Millenials' Internet savvy by explaining how information systems work, not only reviewing how to discern content authenticity but focusing on the relevance of digital information for the task at hand (Borgman, 1996).

But if they are more sophisticated than perhaps librarians are ready to acknowledge, Millennials are also loath to actually visit the library, and understanding the origins of this sentiment is critical to providing effective instruction and services to Millennials. A great deal of research has been undertaken regarding the library habits of secondary school students, and the results are illuminating. Although a clear correlation exists between high-school library use and college library use, in one study, more than one-third of respondents indicated that their school library was open before or after school for three hours or less each week (Kinnersley, 2000). In her examination of college undergraduate library use, Whitmire found that a 'majority of the undergraduates ... did not spend much time in the secondary school library' (Whitmire, 2001: 530). There is little doubt that this early lack of experience inside the library has a long-lasting impact; according to Whitmire, the library experiences of undergraduates was never more than occasional (Ibid., 532). Clearly then, lack of physical access to the library is something that is ingrained in a significant number of students prior to arriving at college or university level. The affect is to minimise (if not marginalise) the importance of the library as a physical space.

Related to this lack of access is the supplanting of the library by the Internet as the information conduit of choice. Related to the limited access to the library is the increasing referral by elementary and secondary teachers to Internet search engines as research tools. In another Pew study, 94 per cent of students indicated they rely upon the Internet for their research needs, 71 per cent indicated that the Internet was their primary source for a 'big project they did for school'; and 87 per cent of parents of those students 'believe the Internet' was helpful to their children's efforts in school (Lenhart, 2001: 5). Following the information habits of earlier grades, in one survey of college students, 79 per cent of respondents indicated they utilise the Internet for all or most of their assignments (Jones, 2002). OCLC's 2005 survey reported that only 2 per cent of college students begin their research using a library website, and only 6 per cent use library resources to validate information.

Thus, academic librarians find themselves working with students who are given to questioning the reliability and value of information, but because of limited access to librarians and libraries, and a reliance on Internet resources, often struggle with more scholarly, rigorous research. And given the size of the challenge – i.e. altering the research habits of these students – students, librarians and teaching faculty must work together to affect any fundamental, long-lasting change.

Given that, at a young age, some students have learned to live without the library (i.e. without physical access to the library), one of the more pressing concerns of librarians is getting students to visit. The advantages to the students should be obvious: areas in which to study, access to computing resources, and easy access to *all* of the library's resources. Even more importantly to students is the accessibility to, and availability of, research experts (i.e. librarians). Indeed, studies have shown that when the need for assistance arises while using online resources 'they prefer face-to-face interaction' with the person providing that help (OCLC, 2002: 5). But it is equally true that most students prefer remote access (i.e. outside the library) to actually going to the library. The question then is how to overcome this internalised barrier to access? According to Whitmire (2001: 537), the 'variables having the strongest relationship with ... academic library use involved their academic activities. Student-faculty and peer interactions, active learning and engaged writing activities ... impacted library use'. Clearly then, collaboration between teaching and library faculty on the creation of writing and research assignments represents the most effective means of motivating students to visit their library.

If there is one shortcoming that most educators possess, it is that they somehow have a monopoly on all the good ideas, or that somehow only they can impart the wisdom necessary for students to move forward educationally and intellectually. However, there is a growing body of literature that indicates otherwise; it is becoming clear that where it has been utilised, 'peer instruction enhanced meaningful learning' (Cortwright, Collins and Dicarlo, 2005: 107). One venue illustrating this point is a 'gateway' research course for psychology majors at California State University Long Beach. The instructor regularly utilises students to lead instruction regarding library resources, specifically the electronic database PsycInfo. The students chosen to lead the instruction first work with the subject librarian to gain an understanding of how to utilise the databases effectively. Multiple training sessions are not unusual, and this underscores a point found in the literature: 'Faculty must be realistic about the amount of time required to learn complex concepts and provide practice time to explore underlying concepts and students must have time to "grapple" with specific information ... thus learning cannot be rushed' (Ibid.,110). So, if peer teaching is to be employed successfully, faculty must provide the time and support necessary for learning to occur. Where faculty members are committed to ensuring the success of peer instruction, the results are encouraging. Indeed, the entire experience of learning from peers enhances the ability of students to interpret, relate and incorporate 'new information with existing knowledge' thereby enabling students to apply 'the new information to solve ... problems' (Ibid.). Finally, and not insignificantly, students indicate that they enjoy the process of learning from peers, which certainly improves the likelihood of embracing and retaining the information provided. If librarians and faculty are committed to changing the information seeking techniques of Millennials (i.e. moving them from an 'Internet first' approach), peer instruction offers one method for doing so.

Of course, there is nothing wrong with tradition, and for some the venerable bibliographic instruction session (a.k.a. information literacy, library orientation, etc.) is the method of choice for information students about the availability and functionality of library resources. Research into the effectiveness of these sessions indicates that students who have attended even a single library session 'cited a greater variety of sources on assignments and reported a greater comfort level with library research than their peers who did not' (Portmann and Roush, 2004: 462). Clearly, then, almost any kind of exposure to library instruction can prove beneficial.

However, it must also be pointed out that PowerPoint and other passive technological aids, are the bane of the active learner's existence – and make no mistake, Millennials are the quintessential active learners. After all, as has been pointed out on more than one occasion, and in more than a single way, 'students these days are more apt to take control of their learning and choose unconventional ... methods to learn better' (Carlson, 2005: 2). This fact, combined with librarians' shared understanding that the bulk of library instruction occurs on a 'one-and-done' basis, should be motivation enough to seek out more dynamic teaching methods.

One instruction methodology that should be incorporated into bibliographic sessions to an even greater degree than is done already is an emphasis on critical thinking. Conventional thinking adheres to a belief that students should be introduced to identifying and utilising information sources prior to engaging in critical analysis of information; but 'it can be argued that critical thinking should precede a knowledge of information sources and retrieval techniques ... critical thinking is surely no less valuable at the outset of the students' studies' (Atton, 1994: 310). Stated another way, the ability to analyse the available resources is fundamental and a logical first step in conducting successful research.

The Millennial generation is one of the most technologically savvy, informationally sophisticated groups to ever pass through academia.

Their instinct to question the reliability and validity of information makes them naturally critical researchers. However, their lack of experience with library resources has left them ill at ease with the tools for scholarly research. Into that generational mix are also technology 'natives' who do not speak the seemingly first language of technology, and whose prior experiences offer entirely different perspectives on academic life and the domain content that they encounter. Knowledge of *all* student subgroups is imperative as reference librarians work with teaching faculty to create critical writing assignments, offer opportunities for peer instruction, and transform bibliographic instruction sessions into critical learning experiences where students can develop their natural abilities at scholarly research.

The rest of the academic student body

Lest one be lulled into the idea that one approach fits all, it is important to realise that today's academic community represents the most diverse group of people in the history of higher education. Even with rising tuition costs, more individuals are entering college than ever before in order to improve their opportunities for success in life. In many societies where post-secondary education was historically available only to the financially and socially elite, now individuals from a wide spectrum of society are considering a college education. With the implementation of the Americans with Disabilities Act 1990, more individuals with special needs are also pursuing post-secondary options. Rising costs for such learning also results in a wider age range of students as many have to work throughout their academic 'career' to pay for it (Astin et al., 2002). In some cases, career advancement depends on continuing education and advanced degrees, so midlife professionals may enter the academic halls, bringing their work experience with them but being clueless about academic library research.

In any one class, the instructor may be teaching local 18-year-olds, international students in their twenties, career-seeking thirties students, re-entry student mothers in their forties whose children are now in school, second-career students in their fifties, and retirement students in their sixties. An even broader mix of people cross the public academic library doorway as the rest of the academic community, as well as teenagers from feeder secondary schools and neighbourhood residents of all ages, use the reference services.

Each generation, as with Millenials, exhibits trends of behaviours and expectations. While individual differences trump any generalisation, some patterns do emerge (Hicks and Hicks, 1999):

- Gen Xers (1966–1980) are individualistic career nomads. Self-starting and resourceful, they seek autonomy and purpose.

- Baby Boomers (1946–1965) are the counter-culture turned mainstream, hard-working citizens who still carry a torch for ideals. Continuing to be competitive (because of their numbers), they seek public recognition before it is too late.

- Traditionalists (born 1945 and before) are retiring after loyal service to a single employer, if possible. They tend to be patriotic (partially because of wartime experience) and conforming in behaviour.

Reference librarians may interact with a mixed group occasionally in instructional sessions, but are more likely to interact with them individually. The issue then becomes one of intergenerational expectations.

When distance education is added to the information-behaviour equation, reference services become even more problematic because of technological and communication barriers. On the technical side, there may be problems with inter-operability, hardware and connectivity limitations, firewalls and other security issues, and co-browser connections (Lupien, 2006). On the human side, the barriers may be subtler. Reference resources and services seem to exist in vacuo, and even real-time reference chats have an out-of-body reality. Not only is video-based reference service still in its infancy for technological and psychological reasons, but even telephone reference service can seem strained when the two parties do not identify themselves personally. While this practice ensures confidentiality and security, it also breeds artificiality. The reference librarian has to go the extra mile by explicitly stating each research step using a comfortable and patient communication tone, be it verbally or in written form. Only with self-exposure will the distance student reveal their age and experience as it is normally not polite for the librarian to ask such personal questions – and they may come to false conclusions if they do ask. Nevertheless, reference librarians can generally make some assumptions about distance learners who use digital reference service: to whit, they typically:

- use technology with comfort;
- motivate themselves;

- learn independently;
- take risks;
- like anonymity;
- value convenience and mobility;
- seem impatient;
- prefer to work online, sometimes because of language or physical barriers (Rettig, 2004).

In any case, it is usually safe for the reference librarian to 'mirror' the approach used by the inquirer (e.g. similar vocabulary level, similar sentence structure, similar level of formality) as long as the overall tone is professional (Minor and Dunning, 2006).

Additionally, with globalisation and distance education, students are more likely than ever to undertake post-secondary study in a foreign country or enrol in an international distance education programme. Although many such institutions offer English language options for courses of study, students may know the English vocabulary of their specific domain only; knowledge of library jargon may be lacking. Libraries attached to institutions need to think carefully about providing second-language reference materials and services for those international students. Even the teaching and learning styles of a different culture may confuse and frustrate students; their research approaches may contradict prior practices as well. Likewise, expectations about the academic library and its services may well reflect the first country's practices but be totally different from the realities of the overseas degree-bearing institution. For instance, the concept of 'free' lending and open access to information may seem strange to some international students. Technology creates another set of barriers, as international students have to deal with information that depends on software unavailable to the distance learner, in addition to deciphering unfamiliar organisation schemes for electronic information retrieval. In short, international students often have to overcome many misperceptions and resolve conflicting educational practices. Reference librarians need to become aware of those barriers to learning, and figure out ways to bridge those international gaps. A few suggestions include:

- using straightforward and literal language, simple sentence structures and present tense;
- contextualising concepts;

- incorporating visual and audio cues;
- building on students' strengths;
- partnering with native language experts;
- modelling positive and patient behaviour (Sarkodie-Mansah, 2000).

In this process, reference librarians have to make sure that they convey a sense of respect for international students whose language might not express the depth of their intellectual knowledge base.

Very few assumptions can be made about this cross-section of information seeking behaviours and needs – except that they vary tremendously. Particularly at the reference desk where librarians are meeting users 'cold', it is impossible to predict what the enquirer brings to the interview. People vary in their perspectives about information itself, reasons for seeking information, the research process, bases for acting on information, and their role with regard to information (Case, 2002). A few dimensions follow:

- *Content knowledge.* Each person comes with a set of experiences and intellectual knowledge about the world, the potential of which has been exponentially expanded because of technology (e.g. television and telecommunications). Nevertheless, basic cultural literacy may be sadly lacking because of limited curriculum and increasing migration. Throughout the world, isolated communities are a thing of the past, and even stable community bases are threatened so that the transmission of social knowledge and wisdom is disappearing. Academic librarians cannot assume that students will know about the Cold War (which is now the name of a rock band) or about the Depression (beyond a mental condition). On the other hand, people may be more globally conscious and exposed to social truths that were hidden in earlier times.

- *Knowledge about libraries.* The person standing in front of the desk may be a librarian in another setting – or an illiterate passer-by. Dress can be deceiving; the long-haired casual guy may be a computer programmer, and the sharp-dresser may be a mortician; both or neither might be library aficionados. A patron may be accustomed to a different library classification system, and just need quick instruction on the academic library's system; another patron may be used to asking for a book because their prior library had closed stacks. Because library quality varies so much from country to country, reference librarians cannot assume that a non-native user is uninformed (or knowledgeable) about reference sources.

- *Knowledge about research.* Most academic librarians assume that entering freshmen know little about research processes – or have uneven experiences. However, some secondary schools do provide strong information literacy instruction and opportunities for research projects. Nevertheless, few incoming students recognise or read scholarly journals or understand the concept of peer-reviewed scholarship. Definitions of research vary wildly, and few older students really understand the term 'information literacy'. In the Google age, subscription databases seem like the library's greatest secret. Furthermore, many teaching faculty do not use specialised library reference tools, and some rely on their teaching assistants to do literature reviews.

- *Knowledge about technology.* Because technology encompasses so many skills and resources, it is safe to say that no one is a technology master. However, it is often difficult to discern areas of technology competence. The retiring gentleman may be an IBM executive; the cell phone addict may be clueless about search engines. Many Millenials are technology proficient on a personal level, but lack research-oriented technical skill. Even within the framework of the Internet, individuals may rely only on free websites, and consider the Wikipedia to be the ultimate resource. Others may use online trade information and scientific datasets regularly, but be unaware of streaming video sources. Until the reference librarian starts interacting with the patron, all technology bets are off.

The lifeline of academia

In examining and addressing the information behaviours and needs of the academic community, it is useful for academic librarians to frame their thinking in terms of the lifelong process of learning and teaching. At each stage, individuals' needs and knowledge base may differ. Broadly speaking, the more advanced the position, the more advanced the potential technological tools and services needed. Nevertheless, personal as well as professional expertise is as varied as each person so usually need to be addressed in such a manner. Emphasis should be placed on the information needs, with technology being a conduit to information rather than the end itself.

As mentioned above, entering freshmen still have one foot in the secondary school and one foot in higher education. Usually, course structures and expectations require significant readjustment for freshmen. Rather than doing nightly homework, students have to pace themselves to read prolifically and write substantial research papers. Students may also be taking courses in subject domains that they have never encountered before: psychology, philosophy, engineering, business, anthropology, communication studies, to name a few. Their baseline knowledge may be nil, so they need foundational resources. Their prior library experiences may have been limited, and most students are overwhelmed by the size and complexity of most academic libraries. No wonder that students may develop library phobia or stick to the familiar encyclopaedia and freely-available websites. In addition, the concept of a reference librarian may be totally unknown to them unless they have frequented good public libraries, and they may have no idea how to approach such a being. Academic librarians need to parse library instruction into several components:

- orientation to library facilities to help students navigate through the stacks;
- orientation to library resources and services, which might be virtual as well as physical;
- general information searching skills such as locating and evaluating information;
- information processing skills such as note-taking, manipulating information, and communicating results.

Undergraduate students continually expand their content and research expertise, depending on their programme of study. As students start to focus on their major specialty, they need to learn how to 'think like a professional', be it a mathematician or a historian. Likewise, they need to be exposed to domain-specific reference sources and research methodologies. At this level, students should consult subject librarians who have deeper content knowledge as well as overall information literacy expertise. Sometimes overlooked are those students transferring from junior colleges who may have experienced little library instruction. A special effort needs to be made by the entire academic community to make sure that these students do not fall in the information literacy gap.

Graduate students frequently attend a different university from the one in which they earned their first degree. Therefore, their previous library experience may not prepare them for the next educational step. Furthermore, most post-baccalaureate degrees require substantial research, which might be a new experience for students. Particularly if they majored in a different subject than for their graduate work (e.g. museum studies, teaching, public administration), they may need to start from square one in terms of reference sources. On the other hand, doctoral candidates may bring sophisticated research agendas. Even more than in undergraduate programmes, the diversity of students can be immense: from young adults to senior citizens. International students are also more likely to be in the crowd than in undergraduate study. Many of these individuals are re-entry students who have not frequented an academic library in literally decades. For academic librarians, the libraries and their resources will, one hopes, have changed to meet current research demands; for the poor student, however, such changes can seem insurmountable. Reference librarians need to practise active listening skills and patience as they ferret out graduate students' questions and existing knowledge base.

Faculty represent another wide range of research expertise and needs for reference sources and services. Full-time teaching faculty are more likely to know and use the library than part-time or itinerate lecturers who commute between teaching engagements, even if it is just for course reserves. On the other hand, because part-timers might acknowledge their lack of familiarity with the library, they may be more apt to ask the reference librarian to explain library resources and services to their classes. As they pursue tenure, faculty may use reference services differently along the way.

- *Beginning faculty* usually focus on their teaching. They may ask the reference librarian to identify available reference resources, suggest relevant subscription databases, help develop course e-reserves, and instruct their students about locating reference materials. Reference librarians should get to know incoming faculty from the start so they can alert these newcomers to library resources and services. Particularly as new faculty often do not have a teaching background, reference librarians can help them design their courses to include information literacy and to take advantage of course management systems. Reference librarians should also ask to examine sample student work to determine whether information literacy instruction has been useful, and whether other interventions need to be pursued.
- Tenure-seeking faculty tend to think about research and publishing. They may ask the reference librarian for lists of domain-specific peer-

reviewed journals, or request hard-to-find studies from other institutions. Savvy faculty develop good professional relationships with subject librarians in order to keep them current on new publishing developments. Subject librarians should take this opportunity to promote current awareness services and selective dissemination of information options, including RSS feeds. Reference librarians should also consider co-authoring research articles and participating in research initiatives, especially as telecommunications can facilitate collaboration in developing documents and conducting research. Of direct benefit to reference and information services, research on information seeking behaviour of the academic community could provide a foundation for systematic attention to information literacy efforts.

- Senior faculty may grow complacent in their use of the library, or delegate research to their junior colleagues or graduate students. Indeed, their information-seeking agendas may have more to do with retirement plans than academic endeavours. On the other hand, this population may be conducting major research studies, and their influence may be international in scope. In any case, reference librarians should not fall into the complacency rut either, but continually look for opportunities to collaborate with these experienced faculty members. Sometimes a new technological reference tool can renew veteran faculty's enthusiasm and engagement.

Support staff and administrators comprise another set of academic community constituents. Administrators, in particular, may be more interested in the behind-the-scenes operations of the library (e.g. facilities, budgets, personnel) than reference services per se. Support personnel, such as learning assistance staff and health clinicians, are often overlooked in terms of library services. Nevertheless, these staffers may call upon the library to conduct background research for campus initiatives or potential policies (e.g. acceptable use policies, wi-fi issues, HIV/AIDS policies, technology literacy requirements); technology-related issues are good grist for the collaboration mill. These individuals may well see research from a service perspective rather than a purely intellectual endeavour. Reference librarians should actively participate in campus committees and other task forces that involve staff and administration so they can contribute their expertise for the good of the institution – and advance the library's mission in the process.

Increasingly, higher education is also seeking partnerships with their local communities. Librarians in these other agencies are natural collaborators with academic librarians, and can provide valuable introductions to community members. Community librarians can also provide useful information about the community – its information needs as well as its reference-related resources. By building relationships with the local community, reference librarians can refer the academic community to knowledgeable experts in the field, and can facilitate the transition of young people and other potential students to their campuses to optimise their lifelong learning success. Web-based information and tutorials can be particularly effective reference tools to share with the community. Deeper collaboration may necessitate discussion about interoperability of systems, security measures and technology-related policies, but the professional relationship must be in place first for such technical details even to be considered.

Over time, reference librarians can get to know the academic community, and develop strong working relationships with them that can bridge changing academic demands and information sources. This potential deep connection can improve reference and information services through long-range collaborative planning and evaluation. Technology can facilitate these information needs and behaviours, but the foundation must be built on interpersonal knowledge and professional relationships that can weather the dynamics of the academic community and outside influences.

2

Technology impact on reference and information services staffing

Henry DuBois and Lesley Farmer

Maria gets to the reference desk just in time; the current librarian is finishing up his session with a middle-aged Latina student. During her two hours, Terri has dealt with course add/drop questions, pointed the way to the reservations desk and the photocopiers numerous times, signed up people with library PIN accounts, located pertinent theses, referred students to the library's online citation style links, helped people find relevant sources using the library OPAC, shown several individuals how to find periodical articles (some peer-reviewed, some within the last year, some print only, one available only on microfiche, one that needed interlibrary loan service), answered two technical questions from faculty by phone, used a Shakespeare concordance, and checked the online educational statistics office for figures on computer use in schools. She knows that e-mails are piling up (she gets about a hundred daily), and she needs to contact the science department to give her input on reinstating a subscription to *Zoological Record*. This week she also needs to review, update and upload her subject Web guide as well as prepare for three class instruction sessions. Terri hears a buzz, her PDA signalling that she has a meeting to attend, on the newest version of the campus's course management system. Terri can safely say that she never gets bored!

Even with the ever-increasing cost of online subscription databases and other digital resources, the greatest expenditure in academic libraries continues to be salaries. Each library staff member represents a significant investment in a unique set of skills and capabilities that fit within the existing mission and structure of the library. With the advent of digital technology, the staffing picture becomes even more complex.

Reference staffing B.D.T. (Before Digital Technology)

For a long time, academic librarian positions have been both specialised, in the sense that librarians need in-depth subject knowledge so they can 'speak the language' of the faculty and students they serve, and they must be 'generalists' who can field many questions about subjects outside their degree specialty. Historically, traditional academic libraries employed more professionals than they do currently. A representative organisational structure consisted of a circulation librarian, an order librarian, a technical services librarian, and several reference departments (science reference, education reference, etc.), each managed by a librarian. Each department might have its own corps of librarians, a department secretary, and student assistants. Librarians were expected to know the sciences or the social sciences or education in depth, but what went on in the other departments was of little interest. Technical services routinely employed several professional librarians who did original cataloguing, and they tended not to interface with the reference staff.

Reference staffing in a technological environment

Generally, reference services have become more in-depth and more stretched because of technology. Explaining how to get to an online database, how its interface works, demonstrating Boolean logic, then helping the student evaluate and organise what he/she retrieves can be challenging, especially given the inadequate research skills and short attention span of many incoming freshmen. On the other hand, few would deny that both intellectual and mundane library activities like completing forms and checking out books have become more efficient and accurate and less burdensome to staff and library users because of technology.

Certainly, it requires a broader and constantly updated set of skills for library staff as new databases, new systems, and new equipment have become the norm. Service expectations on the part of users have increased; 24/7 reference is widespread, and library users are familiar with many other services that can give them information and answers whenever a question comes up; they want no less from the library. Web-based courses are growing in popularity and distance education student populations can be located very far from their 'home' library, yet the library acknowledges a responsibility to serve them.

Nevertheless, the key difference between the traditional and technology-enhanced academic library staff is attitude and aspirations; today's professionals and paraprofessionals need to be excited and energised by a challenge. They are expected to have greater versatility and interchangeability because there are fewer of them, and the organisation needs to be able to deploy its human resources to fit its priorities. Current academic philosophy is that librarians are professionals who have been educated to perform professional functions (teaching, reference and consultation, materials selection, collection organisation, and liaison with students and faculty).

Supervision and management use a different skill set, and many academic library administrators hire well-paid and well-prepared paraprofessionals to perform those kinds of functions. Paraprofessionals also field 'informational' questions in person and by phone in tandem with the reference desk. They offer advice to student researchers on how to locate databases in their field and simple navigation of the library catalogue and website. They refer to the librarian questions about search strategy, choice of a particular database for a particular project, and other matters requiring a higher level of subject expertise or searching skill. At some institutions, the ratio of professional to paraprofessional staff library-wide is about three to one.

Because of the technical complexity of some library functions nowadays, the library also needs to employ highly-qualified technology staff. Often, library directors control fiscal allocations, but they might not have the business experience or staff expertise to handle the technology. Negotiating all those details involves a team of specialised expertise:

- technology strategist;
- technical coordinator;
- software programmer;
- applications specialist (installation, troubleshooting, instruction, maintenance);
- web designer/developer;
- web maintenance expert;

- network manager;
- technical troubleshooter (patches, etc.);
- cabler;
- data entry staff;
- digitisation experts;
- digital rights/licence overseer;
- business comptroller;
- help desk/customer service (J. Horn, personal communication, 2006).

Technology has also increased the use of outsourcing. Some academic libraries outsource processing of new books to services such as OCLC PromptCat. Many have eliminated in-house binding. Library administrators find that it is faster and more cost-effective to have these functions performed outside the library. Furthermore, technology has a role in the selection of outsourcing and other application vendors. Technical systems must coordinate well with existing library management systems in order to make tasks easier for staff and ensure that errors are kept to a minimum. Administrators take advantage of networking with colleagues and of opportunities to learn about new services at professional conferences.

One concrete area that reflects the impact of technology on staffing patterns is technical services. When cataloguing was automated by OCLC, nearly all of those librarians were given 'meaningful reassignments' in areas of librarianship most had probably never considered or expected. In those days librarians were very specialised; if an academic library job opening was announced, the first question would be, 'public or technical?' So the generalist librarian who does instruction and reference and collection development is largely a product of technology and its impact upon technical services. Technical services operations (cataloguing, ordering, receiving, binding/preservation) are now primarily the province of paraprofessionals. In many academic libraries, technical services are exclusively paraprofessional activities, as libraries tend to outsource any cataloguing complex enough to require a professional to do it, such as works in unfamiliar languages. Again, the paraprofessionals have classifications and compensation appropriate to their increased responsibilities and they are expected to know the latest permutations of OCLC and the library's integrated library management system, and to periodically retrain to keep pace with new releases and upgrades. Because professional librarians routinely use the management system for reference services with clientele as well as when developing reference collections, technical services work more closely with reference functions than before.

Indeed, library technology has promoted a much more interdependent relationship among librarians and support staff, and among library organisational units. It forces all library staff to see the bigger picture. Everyone can see when a book is ordered, and track the progress of the order through cataloguing. Everyone can immediately discover alternatives through WorldCat and other interlibrary loan applications for obtaining items elsewhere. Everyone can identify demand and gauge cost-effectiveness of the purchases made for information materials, including databases.

The library organisation is forced to become less insular and more collaborative because of technology. Technical staff may 'intrude' into a library operation to make it more effective and efficient (for example, an automated lost book replacement system). This may cause a little tension with some librarians, as they perceive something that was entirely under their control now being guided by their input, but no longer fully dependent upon them. Staff reactions can and will range from grateful acceptance to uneasiness to paranoia when any new system, procedure, programme, or equipment is introduced.

Hiring staff

Academic library managers hire based on current skills, substantiated by evidence (not just claims) that those skills have been made manifest in their work. They also look for a 'spark', for people who are intrigued and excited by technology, looking for new ways to use it to improve a library's operations or services. While administrators cannot predict what kinds of specific skills will be required in the future, they know that the library will need people who will thrive in an environment of change, new challenges and ambiguity, people who will be eager to learn new skills and will want to keep themselves and their library ahead of the curve. It is not the *ability* to learn; it is a passion for lifelong learning that they want to see. This approach to hiring applies to all levels of library staff, from pagers to managers.

The applicant pool may be quite varied and hard to assess. Library school education tends to be pretty basic (web page creation using Front Page, overview of library management systems and databases) and the best librarian candidates seem to have picked up their most useful experience through a practicum, an internship or in a prior job. Administrators look for evidence of growth and accomplishment in these prior experiences; this kind of background certainly gives an applicant an edge over someone who has just the degree, regardless of the library school's reputation.

The dilemma that often faces library administrators is whether to hire librarians who may be fairly well versed in some technical areas (programming, web development), or 'techies' who know a lot about those areas, but little or nothing about library functions and the academic culture. Generally, the second scenario works best and benefits the library more. Of course, the technical experts who are appointed need to be able to understand the needs of their customers (the librarians, other faculty, staff and students who are using the systems) and they also need to be able to devise and present solutions to their customers' problems in easy to understand, non-technical language. That is a tall order, but libraries need very smart, very skilled individuals who can apply their skills to meet the needs of a specialised academic environment. Not surprisingly, these high expectations can sometimes result in 'raiding' highly-qualified technical staff from other parts of the campus or from other institutions. While this practice enables libraries to get specialists who already have a good grasp of campus resources and operations, it also requires that these technology agents be cooperative and have respect for one another's staff and mission.

Technical expertise and interaction

The question is not whether technological skills are required for a particular information service position, but rather the *degree* to which they are required. Few, if any, library jobs today do not require some computing skills, and those who work at interpreting and explaining the online catalogue to the public, in helping them choose and use online databases, or download and format citations have to be able to use the computer as a tool with confidence and efficiency. The California Library Association (2005) has developed a list of basic technology competencies for reference librarians:

- operate, manage, and troubleshoot desktop computers and associated peripherals;

- create and manipulate documents using productivity software applications;
- use and manage electronic communications;
- use web browsers and associated plug-ins;
- employ electronic-based searching skills;
- comply with copyright laws, including those that apply to electronic resources;
- understand security, filtering and privacy issues on public computers;
- identify and use library electronic resources, including subscription databases, know how to find them outside the library environment, and comply with associated policies;
- instruct clientele in the effective use of library electronic resources.

Academic librarians are routinely expected to construct and manage web pages designed to guide and assist students and faculty in the librarians' assigned subject disciplines. Obviously if they are required to teach others how to use a database in their subject, they must be confident and experienced at using it, especially one that is complex, such as SciFinder Scholar.

It is certainly advantageous for library managers to be technologically informed. Professional reading, attendance at conferences, and networking with colleagues helps keep them current. While they themselves do not need to have high-level technical skills, library administrators need to understand capabilities and trends to be able to work with others to develop a plan that will articulate both short and long-term goals related to information technology.

Librarians and paraprofessional staff look to the technical systems team to support their needs. They call upon a helpdesk to resolve daily problems with office or instructional computing equipment. They submit proposals for equipment, software or programming, requiring a greater investment of resources. The technology strategist alerts library supervisors of functional units about ongoing and planned projects, offers suggestions, asks questions, and helps the library focus and prioritise needs. The librarian web content manager, the serials database expert and the library management system supervisor collaborate frequently with one another and with the tech strategist. This communication is absolutely essential to effective operations; each of these individuals has a skill set that cannot be fully exploited unless the other two are participants. Such collaborative teaming, be it formal or informal, is how libraries must function today.

For any one reference service, a number of technology personnel may be needed. For instance, to support electronic reservation requires a variety of skills:

- scanning into readable formats;
- indexing;
- archiving;
- contracting with reservation program module vendors;
- integrating software with existing library automation systems;
- troubleshooting hardware and software;
- programming user authentification and authorisation;
- maintaining system security;
- training.

In this service, most of the staff members appear to cooperate rather than collaborate, handing off one part of the process to the next person to continue rather than working simultaneously together. However, when initiating or transitioning to a technologically-enhanced service, work groups are often needed. They have to identify the need, brainstorm effective solutions, investigate feasible resources, develop and implement plans, and train others in the service's procedures. This process increases cross-department communication and unifies library services, but it can also raise gaps in expertise or conflicts in priority work. To start e-based reservations, for instance, staff can to make many decisions: database fields and standardisation of record entries (e.g. expressing dates in a standard way), storage policies, licensing agreements, copyright policies (particularly those addressed by the National Commission on New Technological Uses of Copyrighted Works), circulation policies, confidentiality policies, interlibrary loan agreements, public relations and training.

The leader of such work groups or developmental task forces needs to communicate effectively both orally and through writing, and must be a skilled negotiator. Particularly in start-up initiatives, the leader needs to be innovative and flexible, as well as organised and supportive. These days most library leaders must have some technological expertise in order to be credible, and they need to be effective problem-solvers and accountable managers: forward-thinking yet practical (Driscoll, 2003).

Staff development

All academic library staff should have basic technology skills, and some also need in-depth knowledge about OCLC, specific information databases, or specialised applications, such as electronic resource management systems. Nevertheless, specific expectations can change rapidly as technology evolves at an increasing pace. When legacy systems are abandoned, staff either need to learn new skills or consider moving to a different position. Successful librarians take care to keep their knowledge and development updated.

In this same spirit, all library staff need cross-training, learning other operations related to the assignment, so they can respond to questions knowledgeably and can fill in when needed to cover an emergency. This cross-training promotes a less insular organisation and a sense of shared mission within the employee.

Because of the impact of digital technology, staff development has become more diverse, more frequent, and more specialised. Some baseline technology training is usually required of all library staff in order to provide consistent help with basic library reference tools such as library catalogues. Technical systems staff may receive very complex (and pricey) training off-campus because programs and their updates are crucial for library operations. Acquisitions of new systems, which occur more often these days, lead to more frequent training. Such training is usually very specific, limited to the staff who will work directly with the product, although people from several institutions might attend the same training. In turn, those new experts are often expected to train their colleagues. Indeed, in-house staff development is likely to occur informally as well as formally as librarians share good websites or e-mail guidesheets on how to use new subscription databases.

Other staff development may focus on new developments. Vendors may visit the library and demonstrate their products. Likewise, exhibits at professional meetings are a great way to gain exposure to new technology and to ask questions of the vendor representative. Most library staff have used online tutorials, and many have participated in Web or video-conferencing, although paraprofessionals are less likely to have experienced high-tech training. Wikis are becoming a quick way to keep library staff up to date with developments. Technology-based delivery modes show a lot of promise for cost-effective training of library staff on a broader scale.

Few academic libraries systematically involve instructional faculty in staff training in technology, however. Apart from news updates or liaison communications, librarians often do little to keep faculty abreast of new information resources. To ensure that faculty incorporate information and reference services into their practice, librarians should consider offering the academic community an 'academic information technology update' session each term, demonstrating the latest products, showcasing new interfaces, discussing changes being planned for the library portal, and seeking community comments and advice.

Despite the need to be responsive and flexible, library staff are not as fluid as technology. Librarians and support staff are hired with a skill set that meets current requirements and, with luck, that skill set can grow and change over time to remain consistent with the library's needs. The problem is that no one can predict what is around the corner and how adaptable current staff will be to the needs of the future. Yet library employees, like many in the public sector, enjoy a great deal of security. Most institutions have little flexibility to replace and refresh staff who do not themselves choose to move on or retire. The consequence of this is that the organisation cannot respond to technological change as quickly as its leadership might wish. Another predicament is that the staff who are comfortable with technology are besieged by the problems, questions and referrals of their colleagues who are less knowledgeable.

Technostress

The number of articles on the stressed academic librarian has grown in recent years, largely due to both the direct and indirect impact of technology. There are numerous reasons behind this:

- Librarians are expected to keep up with technology, which changes constantly.

- Librarians have to evaluate and compare several formats of reference sources, both for acquisition purposes as well as during reference interactions.

- Librarians have to evaluate the quality of potential online reference sources constantly – in terms of the content and in terms of the user.

- Librarians have to deal with equipment issues: outdated systems, technical and mechanical problems, connectivity, scheduling access to computers.

- Librarians have to deal with software issues: installations, upgrades, software glitches, lack of patron knowledge, hacking.

- Librarians have to teach a very diverse group of patrons how to use technology in order to take advantage of library resources.

- Librarians are asked questions about other campus technology, such as course management systems and administrative technology-based functions.

- While the number of reference question may have declined because of alternative sources of information (such as Google, Wikipedia and online answering services), the difficulty and sophistication of the remaining questions has become more challenging.

- Because of the library's increasing technology, the academic community's expectations for library services have also increased.

- With decreasing budgets, academic librarians have to do more with less.

Moreover, a few academic librarians are technophobic. Most staff predate the Internet.

While hiring new librarians helps the situation pre-emptively if technology is used as a criterion for selection, those same new librarians have other stresses, such as lack of knowledge about the campus and lack of professional library experience. In this situation, veteran academic librarians can mentor new staff. Theoretically, mutual support and collaboration based on each person's expertise can ease stress. However, some librarians do not like to feel inadequate and so may hide their lack of technology from younger colleagues. Likewise, newly 'minted' librarians might not appreciate the knowledge gained over the years by senior staff, and may resent having to 'pay their dues' within the system. Thus, the issue is much more psychological than technological in nature.

Underlying reasons for stress transcend technology. In short, stress 'is how the body reacts to threatening, overwhelming, or challenging circumstances' (American Medical Association, 2004: 55). Controlled stress can stimulate the brain and body in a positive way, but chronic stress can affect one's health. Especially as technology seems endlessly unpredictable, long-term stress can result.

What are some coping techniques for stress? Some approaches are short-term: active listening by peers and supervisors, relaxation techniques, guidesheets for technology directions, scheduled breaks, temporary re-assignment of duties, agreed-upon signals to peers to take over reference tasks for a few minutes. Others solutions require long-term commitment: reinforcement and rewards for technological self-improvement, several options for learning technology at one's own pace, cross-training, job-sharing, ongoing and supportive staff development, women's support groups, ergonomic improvements and stress counselling.

One of the best ways to minimise technostress is effective leadership and management. The work environment needs to be organised, safe and supporting. When the entire library staff share a feasible vision of reference and information service; understand the positive role that technology can play in that vision; plan a realistic strategy to achieve the vision; are given the resources to make that vision a reality; and support each person's efforts in that endeavour, then stress is more likely to be handled in a healthy way.

Technology transition case study

As librarians try to use technology in their collaboration with teaching faculty, they need to have good working relationships with technology service centres. This coordination can be problematic because of fiscal decisions and governance issues. One innovative way to overcome possible obstacles is for the library to assume responsibility for instructional technology, which was the situation at California State University, Long Beach (CSULB). The overriding issue is management, not technology: finding the most effective way to deliver services.

In examining CSULB services, it was noted that the same resources and expertise were needed for both Academic Computing Services (ACS) and the library. Both entities supported the teaching faculty, both provided technology resources and training. In general, ACS's functions – student accounts, web support, course management support, faculty development, training – operated almost independently of one another. The library's management style was more integrated. The total infrastructure was analysed in terms of the functions, personnel, management, facilities and resource allocation. Service surveys provided input from stakeholders. Current practices and needs were identified, with the intent of looking at ways to enhance and improve technology and library services overall. Indeed, closer oversight was needed, particularly as the university's course management system, Blackboard (customised and titled BeachBoard), was growing beyond the faculty's control, with costs rising at the same time as the system seemed to become less stable.

One major issue was physical access. At one point, the library managed a building across campus near the dormitories, which housed technology resources. Over the years, ACS assumed responsibility for that facility (renamed the Horn Center) and its services. As demands for computer and library access increased, it made sense for the library to expand its responsibility again to offer support at that site. Services and servers were consolidated. Horn Center hours were increased to provide more computer and resource access. Meanwhile, technical staff were moved to the library in order to be closer to other functions and to facilitate collaboration.

BeachBoard came under the umbrella of library services so students and faculty could enrich their study and research efforts by more easily accessing and sharing relevant information beyond the textbook. Cross-training was also encouraged in order to provide back-up support. It was not easy to adjust to this kind of interaction and closer attention to details. Job descriptions and skills sets had to be retooled; lines of authority had to be realigned. Commonalities had to be found, and mutual goals had to be clarified. Even though the surface issue was technology, the underlying change was human.

As a result of this combining of efforts, functions became more interdependent and cohesive. Library and Academic Technology Services, as the combined services were renamed, provided seamless academic support to the campus community, from research and instructional design to course delivery and resource use. Library and technical staff both trained faculty and students in these areas, building on each others' expertise. They could also help faculty collaborate with one another through in-house training and resource sharing. By analysing BeachBoard use, library and technical staff could determine resource and service needs. Features of BeachBoard were stabilised and supported, and training reinforced the effective integration of library resources. In sum, technical services staff modelled an integrated approach to teaching and lifelong learning supported by knowledgeable personnel who were all headed together in the same direction.

Global issues

Technology demands on academic library staffing can be daunting for some areas of the world. When academic libraries are considered a new phenomenon, when few if any library or information schools exist within a nation or larger region, when language differences further constrain training opportunities, then academic librarian technological expertise may be non-existent. As mentioned earlier, external technicians might be induced to work in academia, but they still need guidance as to the values and operations of librarianship. If basic librarianship training is non-existent, the results will be disappointing.

The International Federation of Library Associations and Institutions (IFLA) and other similar organisations are committed to improving reference and information services in academic libraries within developing countries through staff training. For instance, in their 2006–07 strategic plan, IFLA's reference and information service section has as its first objective to: 'examine best practices in reference and information services, their organisational framework and staffing component in countries around the world'. They also intend to develop and disseminate guidelines and toolkits to support reference staff development. UNESCO hosts an international libraries portal, which includes discussions about reference service staffing. The Fulbright programme offers opportunities for academic librarians to help their peers in other countries. The American Library Association supports international library faculty exchanges, and their International Sustainable Library Development Interest Group (mainly comprised of returning Peace Corps volunteers) produces training manuals for libraries in developing countries. Government entities are also involved in initiatives to help reference services staffing; for example, the US Agency for International Development provides outreach training for in-country academic librarians. These entities realise the impact of technology, and consider that academic librarians in developing countries may well skip the twentieth century to provide current services unhampered by outdated expectations.

3

Technology impact on reference resources

Sara Sluss and Lesley Farmer

People still need to find answers. What are the peer-reviewed journals in microbiology? Where can I get financial aid? What are the major religions in Botswana? Should marijuana be legitimised? Who founded the League of Nations? How do I cite an interview using MLA?

Where do they go for answers? Where it's convenient, and where there's expert information. First, people, usually. Depending on the age and experience, the Internet or a print source (which can include a telephone directory). This pattern applies to professors as well as freshmen.

Traditionally, a major task in information-seeking was finding information, *any* information. Now it might be asserted that the more critical task is finding the *right* information, which might be hiding in a swamp of misinformation. One core task of reference librarians is to collect, organise, store, and facilitate the retrieval of information. Technology expands the world of information, and brings with it challenges for reference services.

What constitutes a reference collection?

At its core, a reference source is one that is referred to often. Young (1983: 188) defines a reference book as 'a book designed by the arrangement and treatment of its subject matter to be consulted for definite items of information rather than to be read consecutively'. A broader, more relevant definition is provided by Prytherch (2000: 318):

'any material, published work, database, website, etc. which is used to obtain authoritative information'.

Each academic library usually has a collection policy, which should include provisions for reference resources. Libraries vary significantly in defining what belongs in the reference collection. Frequent use is usually the first consideration, particularly in answering user queries. Thus, 'ready references' such as generic dictionaries, encyclopaedias, almanacs, statistical abstracts, atlases, directories, biographical aids and bibliographies are normally found on reference shelves. Subject-specific encyclopaedias and the like are placed at the point of most likely access, which may be in a central reference area or integrated into the subject area part of the main collection, with provisos that the item stay within the facility. Another set of 'candidates' for reference collection consideration are those specialised tools that are difficult to use independently or require interpretation, such as multi-step science sources like ChemAbstracts.

Some libraries promote individual reference desk help while others prefer to focus on information literacy class instruction that is integrated into courses. Likewise, class assignments also shape the collection, in that 'factoid' trivia hunts may call for a larger reference collection, as opposed to term papers that would use a wide variety of resources independently, in which case some reference tools might be reassigned to the general collection. With the advent of widespread electronic reference formats, traditional reference collections have tended to become leaner and more focused; while the overall number of reference interactions has declined, the breadth and depth of queries have increased. Furthermore, automated library management systems make it easy for librarians to change locations and circulation policies for reference materials in response to user information-seeking patterns.

Lifecycle management of digital resources

Projects should plan for the lifecycle management of digital resources, including the initial assessment of resources, selection of materials and digital rights management; the technical questions of digitising all formats; and the long-term issues of sustainability, user assessment, digital asset management and preservation. (University of Glasgow

Humanities Advanced Technology and Information Institute and The National Initiative for a Networked Cultural Heritage, 2002).

Collection selection

Regardless of the size of the reference collection, evaluating a possible reference resource requires considering a number of criteria beyond those associated with general selection. For example, academic collections usually strive for a variety and balance of perspectives; their reference materials have to meet a higher standard of objectivity. Here are the basic criteria used for reference materials in general, as suggested by Katz (2001):

- *Purpose*: Is the purpose clear, and does the author fulfil the intended purpose?
- *Authority*: What are the author's qualifications and publisher's reputation? How objective is the content?
- *Scope*: Is the scope well-defined and well-addressed? Is the information current? Does it fulfil a need within the existing reference collection?
- *Arrangement*: What is the sequence of information? What are the features of its indexing and other points of access?
- *Ease of use*: Is the writing clear? Do headlines and layout features facilitate finding the information needed? Do charts, tables and diagrams clarify information? Can the potential audience use the resource independently?
- *Audience*: Does it contribute to the library's and institution's mission? Does it address the needs of the academic community?

Of course, cost and availability also affect selection decisions.

In considering electronic reference resources, format is critical. Even the most cost-effective item is worthless if the equipment and connectivity for using it are prohibitively available (a situation that might occur in developing countries). Beyond the content criteria, additional physical criteria should be considered:

- Interface: How easily can the user find the information needed? What navigation tools are available? Is searching – and metasearching – intuitive and universally accessible? To what depth can the user search for information (e.g. chapter, topic, paragraph, chart)? Is the Help function readily available? Does the source employ an open URL standard? To what extent does the user have to 'bend' to technical formats – as opposed to the technology being crafted to meet user needs?

- *Readability*: Are text and images easy to view? Are additional plug-ins necessary? Is content accessible for individuals with special needs? Can viewing options be changed? This factor is often at the bottom of reference librarians' list as they can usually overcome visual obstacles as they work with their constituents.

- *Functions*: To what extent can content be downloaded, printed, saved or sent?

- *Technical requirements*: What kind of system requirements (e.g. operating system, platform, speed, RAM, video, sound) and connectivity are required to mount the resource? Can the resource be networked? (Many institutions will not consider non-web-based reference products). What impact will multiple simultaneous user access have on performance? What are the details of the licensing agreements (e.g. number of systems, access parameters, service, subscription fees, etc.)?

- *Licensing agreements*: Farb and Riggio (2004) list basic elements of most contracts: scope, completeness of content, duration, warranties, indemnification, access, confidentiality, sharing, archiving, disability compliance, and usage statistics. Increasingly, libraries are considering 'leasing with an option to buy' licences as a way to ensure access through backfile ownership; licensing a database with no right to the content beyond the date of the licence is no longer attractive.

Technology has the potential to help all individuals gain physical access to reference materials. Thousands of reference resources are available in at least two formats: print and electronic. Cost and space enter into the decision, but accessibility is another factor as well. The Digital Accessible Information System (*http://www.daisy.org*) has developed international open standards with the intent that 'all published information, at time of release to the general population, be available in an accessible, highly functional, feature rich format and at no greater cost, to persons with print disabilities'. The consortium also provides open source tools to help publishers and librarians produce and convert material for inclusive use.

Technology not only constitutes a set of formats to consider for acquisition or access, but also provides a rich source of reviews.

Librarians can also look at other collections and ask their professional colleagues for advice more easily now because of the Internet and standard protocols that facilitate transfer of information. They can also set up listservs, e-mail address lists, or online request forms to garner requisition information from the academic community.

Access development

Recently, the term 'access development' is coming to replace, or at least complement, 'collection development', as academic librarians have to determine the status of the reference sources to be used by the academic community. How important is it to own the material? In a digital world, users are often unaware of where information resides – and they don't care; they are just interested in accessing it dependably. On the other hand, many 'old guard' librarians may be more focused on collection maintenance and presentation. New business models for databases force a choice between access and control, where librarians want *both* options. Without any option to buy, librarians are left in a precarious position in terms of their mission.

A presumption persists that geography matters because proximity and convenience have always mattered. The Internet has served to level access, but the academic community is only midstream in experiencing the full impact of this process. Does living hundreds of miles from the collections matter? Not with online databases. This new reality is good news for distance learners and distance education providers. In fact, the definition of distance will need to be redefined or ignored. And why does it ultimately matter? In short, electronic reference providers have elevated the discussion among librarians and preservationists by removing the distance question and making the question be fully about access. Ownership, when copyright does not make it a closed system, becomes trading rights.

Infrastructure

Key to developing electronic reference collections, as with any format, is knowing what information is needed by the target population. However, it is evident that equipment and connectivity is required in order to access electronic resources. In fact, this technology-based issue raises a dramatic tension; do infrastructure demands drive the collection, or do collection needs drive the infrastructure development? For example, academic libraries would all use Macs if Macs were the platform on which academic publishers were building. Therefore, one of the first tasks when considering which electronic reference sources to collect is to identify the technological infrastructure required to support the resources and services. Unfortunately, small independent publishers may become victims in this consideration as products are often expected to be adaptable to future changes in access, policies and technologies. Some of the parameters include:

- terminal/workstation requirements: processing speed, RAM and ROM storage, drivers, video and sound capacity, input/output ports, peripherals;
- system platform(s) for standalone and networked workstations or terminals;
- electrical demands: outlets, power supply, surge protectors, cabling;
- network hardware: servers, routers, hubs, cables, switchers, and the like;
- Internet connectivity issues: cabling, fibre optics, dish, wi-fi, and the like;
- administrative software: security, firewalls, authentification and authorisation, and the like.

Moreover, it is important to determine which of these factors are unique to the library staff facilities and sphere of influence, which need to be communicated or aligned with other parts of the campus, and which are dependent upon other campus offices, such as facilities, financial affairs or academic computing services.

Collection processing and maintenance

Theoretically, technology can help the ordering process. For instance, digital 'wish lists' can be repurposed into purchase orders. Increasingly, as digital orders progress through campus and vendor checkpoints, electronic reviews and signatures can make for seamless tracking *if* all the stakeholders have compatible programs and can agree on the logistics and legalities of such transactions. MARC records can also be incorporated into this process, with the feature of downloading them into the library management system upon arrival of the document. At this point, technology is less of an issue than business agreements.

This convenience comes with a price. Some professionals have a hard time trusting vendors to select, deselect and manage on behalf of academic librarians. Academic cataloguers are likely to assert that outsourcing has resulted in declining cataloguing standards. Recent decisions, such as those negotiated when OCLC and RLG merged, reinforce this attitude. The fact that the Library of Congress would no longer support their name authority file came as another shock to academic librarians.

With physical items, once acquired there was an unstated commitment (barring certain collection rules) to maintain the item for posterity, even in the smallest of libraries. This commitment might define the database as stolid as a book on a shelf. Particularly if electronic resource access is leased, more frequent reconsideration is likely to occur; if the academic community does not use the resource within the licensing timeframe, then that resource might not be renewed. If, on the other hand, libraries wish to keep their electronic references, technology might not support this decision as systems crash to upgrade their software and hardware. Academic libraries may well be more vulnerable in terms of reference collections and their access because of technology. In the final analysis, mission must be absolutely defined; not everything will be (or should be or can be) preserved by every organisation choosing to provide access at some juncture. There must be last copy provisions and agreements, and last copy must include the electronic format. The LOCKSS project (Lots of Copies Keep Stuff Safe: *http://www.lockss.org/lockss/*), an initiative of several universities, facilitates this preservation process.

Technology-based reference sources

Academic libraries are increasingly considering the possibilities of digital libraries. By putting reference resources online, librarians can expand access exponentially, offering reference sources beyond the library walls to remote locations, thus providing more equitable educational experiences for distance and physically challenged learners. Middleware programs such as Lift Transcoder (*http://transcoder.usablenet.com/tt/*), which 'translate' textual material for the visually impaired, further facilitate access to useful reference materials. Especially when digital libraries are complemented with real-time digital reference services, academic librarians can maintain their role as information mediators.

One of the most influential global initiatives relative to reference resources in academia has been the International Conference on Digital Libraries. Some of the major topics under discussion include multilingual information retrieval systems, metadata standards, copyright issues and information sharing.

Websites

Many academic libraries now consider websites as another form of reference resource. In some cases, the same independent document is available in print and online formats. In other cases, websites have replaced a traditional print form of ready reference information. Currency converters, for instance, are best found on the Internet because of their calculation feature, and because information has the potential to be updated instantly.

Many academic library web portals include a Webliography of 'ready reference' sites. Here are some representative university reference websites:

- Australian Catholic University: *http://dlibrary.acu.edu.au/library/elreference.htm*
- Princeton University: *http://www.princeton.edu/~pressman/genref.htm*
- University of Minnesota: *http://www.lib.umn.edu/site/reference.phtml*
- University of Paris: *http://bib.univ-paris1.fr/signets/ref.htm*
- University of Texas at Austin: *http://www.lib.utexas.edu/refsites/*
- University of Waterloo (Canada): *http://ereference.uwaterloo.ca/*

Some academic libraries prefer to provide a short list of reference metasites or directories that link to relevant reference-oriented websites:

- Librarians' Internet Index: *http://www.lii.org*
- Internet Public Library: *http://www.ipl.org*
- Library Spot: *http://www.libraryspot.com/*
- Open Directory Project: *http://dmoz.org/Reference/Libraries/Library_and_Information_Science/User_Services/Reference_Services/Virtual_Reference_Desk/*

- University of Exeter (UK): *http://www.library.ex.ac.uk/internet/uklibs.html*, which links to other UK higher education research libraries

LibWeb (*http://lists.webjunction.org/libweb*) links to 7,500 library servers around the world, including academic libraries, and LibDex (Library Index) is a searchable database of 18,000 libraries worldwide (*http://www.libdex.com/*).

In other libraries, subject librarians maintain mixed-format bibliographies that include a few reputable websites used by researchers in the field, such as the CIA World FactBook (*https://www.cia.gov/cia/publications/factbook/index.html*) for political studies. Some subject librarians routinely catalogue websites in much the same way as any other library resource, a prime example of that practice being the University of Riverside Library (*http://infomine.ucr.edu/reference*).

Virginia Tech University maintains a thorough bibliography of documents to help evaluate Internet sources (*http://www.lib.vt.edu/help/instruct/evaluate/evalbiblio.html*).

Providing reference websites demonstrates a value-added reference service when academic librarians select sites that meet their constituents' academic needs. However, such endeavours can be very time-consuming: selecting, processing, organising and disseminating websites. Furthermore, those URLs need to be reviewed regularly as domain addresses change and site managers might not be timely updaters themselves. Increasingly, initiatives for linking to reference websites are being either outsourced or done via consortia.

Databases

The term 'database' can be confusing when talking about academic reference services. The structure of an electronic database may refer to several kinds of reference sources:

- library management systems, particularly the library catalogue of resource citations;
- bibliographies and indexes that serve as citation databases, such as *National Geographic Index*;
- in-house or other customised databases of resources, such as a directory of local community information centres;
- aggregates of e-books, such as the Oxford online reference library;

- subscription databases that electronically aggregate and index periodical articles, such as ERIC.

It is not surprising that the academic community as a whole might remain a bit mystified. Users have a hard enough time trying to differentiate a library catalogue and a library portal; their ideal system would be one that would harvest all library (and library-accessible) resources into one metasearch query. This approach is being explored as metatagging efforts are improving; one good example is Metascholar, Emory University's digital library research initiative (*http://metascholar .org*).

In most cases, however, academic librarians apply the term 'database' to online subscription databases because those resources are central to research. Increasingly, libraries are shifting to this online periodical option to address several problems:

- space limitations;
- missing issues and volumes of periodicals;
- single simultaneous access to a print copy;
- course reserves labour;
- equity of access for distance learners;
- copyright negotiations when creating course 'readers' (i.e. anthologies of articles).

Calculating total cost can be complex as it involves issues of space, labour (e.g. billing, licence negotiating, processing, filing, reserves, interlibrary loan, etc.), indexing, networking, and programming. From the users' perspective, however, all of these considerations make little difference. Students are currently unlikely to visit the library in order to use print guides to periodicals. In effect, academic libraries are playing catch-up with Google.

Selecting a collection of subscription databases can be a daunting task for academic libraries. The *Gale Dictionary of Online, Portable, and Internet Databases* (*http://library.dialog.com/bluesheets/html/bl0230 .html*) covers more than 15,000 database and database products in all subject areas produced worldwide by more than 4,000 database producers. By that count, typical US academic libraries are likely to subscribe to just one per cent of the potential number of databases. Obviously, selection is based on knowledge about the academic community, the curriculum and research endeavours. Most fields rank the significance of periodicals in their domain; librarians can use this as a checklist when looking over the publications included in each database – as well as comparing the overlap between vendors' products. Online catalogues simplify the selection process, in that librarians can compare their subscriptions with those of similar institutions.

Buying books and journals does not add up to the cost of investment in a single database, and access issues are different. Major technical aspects of databases to be critiqued include:

- ease of use (and help screens);
- browsing and searching features (date range, format choice, 'wild cards', etc.);
- metasearching options (i.e. searching multiple databases simultaneously);
- indexing quality;
- layout clarity, appropriate use of graphics, presentation of results;
- output features: selecting, downloading, saving, e-mailing, exporting;
- accessibility for individuals with special needs;
- system requirements: platform, RAM, speed, network options, Z39.50, open URL compliance;
- vendor reliability, stability, accessibility, service;
- licensing agreements: static vs. dynamic IPs, number of simultaneous users, server options (IPs are still the norm as campus portals make single sign-on a possibility so IP is established earlier in the path, but credentials are still established).

To facilitate database selection, checklists can be used to make sure that all relevant requirements are addressed. See the Appendix for a representative example checklist.

Most database vendors are well established; fewer start-up companies seem to be on the horizon. In recent years, several database vendors have merged into virtual conglomerates. In the process, they sometimes develop 'libraries' of databases or merge them. In the former situation, vendors sometimes create a search 'shell' that incorporates the different databases, but in other situations the unique controlled vocabulary and searching interface of each database is maintained, which can seriously hamper the user's ability to find the information needed. Increasingly, vendors have tried to improve consistency across the individual products that they offer, but if the database does not contain the necessary functionality (e.g. it was created without the benefit of ISSN), then retrofitting becomes prohibitive. Unfortunately, librarians have little control in this decision (although professional organisations *do* liaise with vendors for better service), and generally do not make financial decisions based on these irregularities if the resources themselves are unique and useful to the academic community served.

Systems or consortia of academic libraries can influence database selection and access significantly. Groups can evaluate databases using common criteria, negotiate deep discounts because of their collective user base, facilitate federated resource sharing, and coordinate associated training. The downside of consortia is critical mass: a large enough number of subscribers to make a contract valid. In addition, smaller publishers and niche markets usually cannot afford to negotiate group discounts. On the local library level, a certain tension exists between standardised practices and attention to unique campus demographics. For example, administrative functionality must be considered. How much control does the local administrator have to modify database features to suit local demands, or is the library locked into a single interface? Can the database produce counter compliant statistics for cross-comparison evaluation? Academic librarians need to be able to exploit all databases as fully as possible.

With the advent of full-text subscription databases, locating relevant articles requires fewer steps – though not usually the one-step process that many students might prefer. Libraries subscribe to multiple database products in order to cover the needs of their constituents, users have to figure out which database is best suited to the information task at hand. Increasingly, reference librarians create topical lists of relevant databases and also instruct the academic community in their application. Librarians also need to explain how database searching interfaces work: what are the typical protocols, and what features (such as controlled vocabulary) might vary between databases. Using Boolean search strategies continues to be difficult for neophytes, and locating the actual article can still be confusing if not all citations include the full text. As a cost-saving device, libraries are incorporating software mini-programs that search all the databases for full-text versions of the articles so that duplicative full-text subscriptions are minimised. The disadvantage of this programming is that the academic community needs to be taught how to use the feature, which can be constant demand.

Technology also affects the launching of new databases. Information about each product can be codified and entered into the library's electronic resource management program, to be plugged into an interface that connects with the purchase history, vendor details, and so forth; essentially, librarians can build a record that holds all of the information needed by all members regarding that resource. Such a technological solution is quite 'slick', but it takes substantial effort to launch because the program has to be tailored for local circumstances.

E-documents

Project Gutenberg represents an early attempt to broaden access to documents; their website (*http://www.gutenberg.org*) proclaims that the project is 'the first producer of free e-books'. Since 1971, volunteers have manually digitised print public domain materials, and submitted them to the project for electronic dissemination. At this point, 17,000 items are available, including a few dictionaries, encyclopaedias, and statistics. Other examples of free e-book disseminators who include reference sources follow:

- *http://www.free-ebooks.net/reference.html*
- *http://www.ebookslibrary.com/Reference_EBooks/*
- *http://www.memoware.com*
- *http://textbookrevolution.org/links/useful-reference-tools-and-free-books-that-arent-textbooks.*

While e-book 'readers' still have not caught on in most places, students in particular like to download e-books onto their personal digital devices, including 'smart' telephones. It should be noted that most of these suppliers are private groups separate from libraries; in that respect, Digital Book Index (*http://www.digitalbookindex.org*) stands out because it serves as a federated metasite to the digital collections (including about 2,000 reference materials) of academic libraries around the world.

Reference e-book collections (e.g. Netlibrary, ABC-CLIO, Safari, Ebrary, Books 24/7) are still searching and competing for their niches. If they were geared more toward library selection processes (e.g. cherry-picked for local needs), then they would be adapted more seamlessly into libraries. As it stands, too many providers sell collections with update cycles that may or may not meet local needs. As with databases, reference e-books raise the buy or lease conundrum. Particularly as most reference e-books have access limits, such as a single simultaneous viewer, and contracts for e-books do not always allow for reserves, libraries do not use reference e-books as a general rule. Certainly, most students would not be happy with such one-person access.

Academic librarians tend to look at two resource extremes when purchasing reference e-books: classic works such as the Oxford Collection that the library would want as a whole; and more ephemeral works, especially in technology, as represented by collections such as Safari and Books 24/7. Such specialised materials generally have a short shelf-life in keeping with the industry's changing practices. Another e-book arena consists of government documents; in the USA, federal documents are increasingly being published in electronic form only. For those institutions designated as governmental depository libraries, service providers give the library both the MARC records and electronic document, which can then be incorporated into the library's automated resource management system.

Resource sharing

Although academic libraries try to collect the reference resources that are most useful for their clientele, with the proliferation of information and the limitations of budgets, it is impossible to provide *all* available reference materials. Libraries have shared resources for decades. Library systems routinely move materials between facilities. Union catalogues have facilitated knowledge about other libraries' collections – as well as showing cataloguing practice. In the digital era, the possibilities for sharing resources have grown exponentially. In the same breath, the technological aspects that librarians need to resolve also increase. Detailed information exchange standards need to be established. Resource sharing can be threatening because librarians may fear loss of control, so well-established professional relationships should be in place before tackling the technological challenges of such collaboration.

Some of the typical services include:

- *Borrowing privileges*: Academic libraries and cross-type library systems can develop agreements about borrowing privileges. If an institution belongs to a system that electronically shares a student/faculty database, then accounting can be facilitated. Sometimes online resources may also be accessed from remote locations when the borrower is set up with the library's patron database; the automated management system authenticates and authorises the patrons, and determines their level of access.

- *Interlibrary loan*: WorldCat, system or consortia union catalogues, and other Z39.50-compliant catalogues facilitate searching for holdings in other libraries. Increasingly, librarians and their clientele can search multiple catalogues simultaneously, and reserve the desired volume in one set of procedures. Agreements between systems can result in regular delivery service to the requesting institution.

- *Direct requests*: Consortial partnerships make direct requests and consortial access can blend seamlessly so that the person initiating the request does not need to understand the path. Increasingly, the academic community uses electronic request systems, which are routed to the interlibrary loan office. This system facilitates locating and delivering documents in a variety of formats because of the standardised database field entries. For periodical article requests, library staff routinely e-mail a digital version from their online database, or they scan the article into digital form first; in both cases, the document can be sent directly to the requestor. With electronic formatting, materials are less likely to be damaged or lost, yet access has been broadened. To ensure equity of service, libraries use technology to keep track of requests and are reimbursed periodically to balance the loan 'trade.'

- *Consortia access*: To benefit from group discounts, academic library systems and other library groups negotiate with vendors to acquire or subscribe to reference materials, increasingly in digital format. Users must belong to one of the participating institutions; a software program checks for eligibility, and provides the electronic 'certificate' for access. Policies are created by the consortia, and each site either signs off on the policy, or chooses not to participate in the initiative. Web mark-up languages and computer interchange protocol standards have facilitated these group investments. In the USA, 46 states have agreements with subscription database vendors to provide electronic resources to most educational institutions, with the cost being underwritten by the government.

- *Repositories*: The idea of federated repositories can be very appealing. Each library collects and describes unique publications. The document is stored in a local service, and the metadata record is kept in an in-house database. The metadata are then uploaded into a joint relational database that 'points to' the publication's server (Martin, 2006). The IMS Global Learning Consortium and the Coalition for Networked Information (McLean and Lynch, 2004) have been identifying common functions based on existing standards that can be used across systems to create and use a common interface. With these agreements, access management and searching protocols can be performed on the reference assets seamlessly. While technology advances have made discussion feasible, the implementation of such initiatives will depend on human negotiations and trusting relationships.

4

Technology impact on packaging reference and information

Lesley Farmer

An international studies class assignment requires students to find fourteenth to sixteenth-century maps in order to compare Muslim and Christian perspectives. No documents exist in the library's map room. The map specialist, though, provides the librarians and instructor with a pathfinder to facilitate searches. The strategies not only include likely library catalogue and search engine key words, but the librarian also creates webliographies (easily located using tinyurl) on medieval maps, Arabic maps, and Arabic geography.

Academic librarians have a deep respect for the entity they call information. They value the ideas that the creators set forth, and acknowledge the significance of the 'container' of that information, be it physical or electronic. As any cataloguer knows about hardback vs. paperback vs. digital versions of a novel – let alone illustration variations, abridgements, revisions, and so forth – form impacts function. The new Functional Requirements of Bibliographic Records guidelines codify those relationships, and provide an intellectual concept map of the development and manifestation of ideas and information.

Furthermore, academic reference librarians gleefully delve into those containers. They love to ferret out factoids, compare entries, extract relevant charts, and choose signature art examples. They produce bibliographies about whole documents (including websites) as well as items within them, such as 'book lover quotes'. They create web portals that link the user to pre-selected sources.

Nevertheless, academic librarians tend not to deconstruct those containers, or disembowel ideas from their documental entities. They store and retrieve, but they do not change the information as it is presented. They tend not to be anthologists. They tend not to create information.

That mentality has been shifting. Academic reference librarians *have* produced publications: library histories, research studies, information literacy tutorials, and the like. With the advent of electronic publications, producing and *packaging* information has become more common. Digital formats facilitate repurposing the same information, morphing an outline into a PowerPoint presentation or hyperlinked web page, as needed. As long as the information sources are credited ('anchoring' it) and intellectual property rights are observed, academic librarians are seeing advantages of combining and synthesising ideas/information per se as a value-added service for their users. They are thinking in and across boxes.

The reference librarian as information packager

Reference librarians support the intellectual life of their academic community: in instruction, research and service. Each aspect of the academic life can benefit from information packaging by reference librarians. This set of value-added tasks reveals the subject-based and process-based expertise of information professionals.

Organising information

The most traditional packaging that reference librarians do is *organising* existing sources of information in response to academic community demands. The end product may take the form of a bibliography, a course 'reader', a reserve shelf, or simply a cart of relevant materials. Ideally, the subject librarian and associated teaching faculty collaborate on identifying resources appropriate for a course overall. These items tend to include introductions to major topics, domain-specific subscription databases, and web directories. At this level, the instructor and librarian can create a course bibliography and establish e-reserves to support the entire term. At the learning activity stage, the subject librarian can help the instructor design activities that enable students to understand and apply content-specific learning outcomes. In such a manner, relevant resources can be identified and incorporated: from conceptual introduction to independent practice. These unit or concept-sized compendia of materials can include more narrowly-defined topics. Both parties can seek advice from their peers to provide current, relevant titles, a task that can be accelerated through telecommunications. Likewise, existing electronic bibliographies can be consulted and merged to create course-specific relational databases linking similar courses or programmes of study. When course readers are developed, managing necessary copyright permissions can be facilitated through electronic submission to a copyright permission centre. More typically, the subject librarian enters the instructional design process at the point at which the instructor assigns students their learning activity. It is hoped that the subject librarian receives the student handout or directions ahead of time in order to alert and advise librarian colleagues, but the usual reality is that whoever is managing the reference desk immediately after the course students are dismissed from class is the person who finds out about the assignment. Even at that late point, the reference desk librarian can alert the library staff about the assignment, pointing out feasible resources. Staff e-mails and listservs, as well as assignments on reference desktop electronic 'folders', can save time and frustration for the variety of staff on 'frontline' reference duty.

The reference librarian is sometimes overlooked as a significant research partner. Particularly at the step of reviewing the existing literature, subject librarians bring domain-specific as well as information-seeking expertise. Librarians may also be aware of data collection and analysis tools that can facilitate research impact. The library's users – and the broader arena of information seeking and sources – can also serve as an excellent study population for studies. When pursuing outside research grant funding, faculty would do well to involve reference librarians in their proposals – and librarians need to build authentic academic relationships leading to collaborative research endeavours. Ideally, each discipline should have a subject reference librarian liaison who can work in proactive collaboration with them, providing ongoing information about new resources and services to meet research interests.

In service to their institutions, reference librarians can play a significant role in campus committees by organising group documents and relevant sources in support of campus initiatives. In some cases, librarians may be conducting background research using the existing library collection or other accessible materials; in other cases, librarians may be harvesting institutional documents that reside in library special collections, in other offices on campus, or on institutional servers. In this latter scenario, acquisitions librarians can use this situation to discuss the possibility of the library establishing an organisational collection of documents as a means towards managing knowledge systematically. Particularly when accreditation agencies examine the viability of institutional programmes, having a librarian organise evidence into an accessible database can make a significant difference in the review process. Librarian expertise should also be considered when indexing college catalogues in order to optimise access to institutional information.

Synthesising information

A step up from organising information is *synthesising* information. This latter process may involve locating and extracting information within sources. Usually, information found in various sources is compared in order to reveal patterns. At this level of engagement, the reference librarian might make critical judgments as to the validity and significance of source material. Other examples of synthesising information include:

- choosing the top ten resources on a topic;
- providing abstracts about relevant sources;
- creating a table highlighting the key points of relevant source content;
- developing a multimedia presentation about major research findings on a topic;
- providing domain-specific research study updates.

Reference librarians routinely synthesise information about *processes,* typically those related to information literacy. As they observe and work with library users, reference librarians often discover trends in information seeking behaviours, for instance. They may identify key research bottlenecks, and also identify effective interventions to help the academic community have a successful research experience. In these situations, the information does not reside in a resource per se but rather reflects the result of data gathering and analysis. It should be noted that technology can help collect unobtrusive data via subscription database usage statistics, computer searching histories, online digital reference transactions, among other means. Based on such data, reference librarians may create documents that help the academic community learn how to complete information tasks independently: research guides, multimedia presentations, web tutorials, and so forth.

This labour-intensive reference service might be in response to instructor queries, but it might also be done as a collaborative project with teaching faculty. Such synthesising projects are sometimes funded by grants or constitute part of an institution's internal research or administrative improvement plans. Technology can facilitate this process in several ways:

- using content analysis software (e.g. Atlas-ti, Nudist, Nvivo);
- creating digital display tables;
- using graphic organiser software (e.g. Inspiration, MindMapper, PiCoMap) to display trends;
- reusing content between software productivity tools (e.g. word processors to authoring tools);
- disseminating the synthesised document electronically.

In any case, the reference librarian must possess credibility and a trustworthy reputation for these products to be requested *and* accepted. Normally, such synthesising activities involve collaboration, which can also benefit from telecommunication tools.

Interpreting information

Interpreting information requires in-depth content knowledge. Nevertheless, reference librarians are frequently asked to make judgment calls about information, particularly if the requester has little background in the subject matter. Probably the most 'popular' topic is copyright information; reference librarians are often assumed to be copyright experts, and may be asked if academic practices comply with fair use guidelines. Thus, librarians have to interpret both the law as well as the copyright implications of intended practice. Reference librarians need to be very careful when they interpret information as they might be held liable for the advice they give. For that reason, most reference librarians refer such interpretive queries to experts in the field. Nevertheless, in those areas where reference librarians *do* possess specialised knowledge, they might well create documents that interpret information for use by the academic community – such as ways to comply with copyright. Probably the greatest use of technology in interpreting information lies in consulting experts and expert information to validate the interpretation. The final presentation of the interpretation might also incorporate technology, as the reference librarian determines the most effective format and means to share their interpretations.

Information advocacy

A newer role for reference librarians is information advocate. This social activist role reflects the reference librarian's belief that the entire academic community and beyond need access to information. A couple of areas that are obvious issues for information advocacy include health, diversity and safety. For example, students can be surprisingly naïve about safe sex practices or public hygiene issues. Students who are exploring their sexual identities may find it hard to locate affirming or objective information. Students should be aware of their citizenship duties and options, such as selective service and voting information. What rights do non-citizen students and faculty have? Reference librarians can identify needed information, or they might respond to the needs as identified by other academic community entities, such as international studies or the health centre. Ideally, academic librarians should participate in institutional initiatives that cross offices, so that reference services can contribute to group goals. Some of the specific tasks that reference librarians can do in information advocacy include:

- identifying needed information, such as immigration guidelines;
- identifying possible academic community entities that can address the information need;
- locating relevant information from library, institutional or other resources;
- selecting the 'best' information in light of target audience needs, considering depth of information needed, language, reading level, format, timeliness;
- synthesising information;
- organising and packaging information for effective dissemination;
- making a concerted effort to make sure that such information is made easily available.

As with the other aspects of packaging information, technology can affect information advocacy, from identifying needs to determining the format of presentation and dissemination. For example, online institutional surveys can reveal informational needs. Even circulation and interlibrary loan statistics can identify areas of need, either because certain topics have high circulation or because certain topics are requested frequently. As information advocates, reference librarians should also be sensitive to equity access issues so that those individuals with limited technological ability will have ways to obtain the information, and those individuals with physical constraints will be accommodated in their search for needed information.

Technology-enhanced information packaging elements

As mentioned before, academic reference librarians have packaged information for decades as they continue to think of ways to facilitate access to it. With the advent of digital technology, creating and repurposing information packages have never been so widespread and sophisticated. Particularly as digital content can be transferred between applications and customised based on specific needs, academic librarians can systematically develop and deploy a collection of technology-enhanced information packages.

Content

Information packaging efforts can be classified by the focus of their development and dissemination intent.

- *Library-centric*: These information packages tend to reflect three realities: library news, library 'curriculum', and 'ready-made' answers to stock questions. Examples of the first include announcements about recent acquisitions and new services, changes in library facilities that might affect users, and changes in technology (e.g. different interfaces, protocol changes, connectivity improvements). Information literacy-related packaging helps users interact with information more effectively. In one sense, such guidance acknowledges and anticipates user needs, based on prior experience. In another sense, though, teaching faculty might think that the library is 'pushing' some arbitrary agenda, so it is important for reference librarians to explain that information literacy standards and processes are the result of careful analysis of user information behaviours across academic domains. The third library-centric package, 'ready-made information' immediately benefits the library staff who have to answer the same questions repeatedly over time. These stock answers may take the form of subject-specific bibliographies, FAQs, tutorials, and process presentations. Many of these library-centric packages are developed as part of a long-term reference plan, although some packaging of information can be the result of an unexpected crisis, such as a natural disaster. Librarians may also create information packages on a 'just in case' basis, such as plans in the case of a terrorist attack. Ideally, reference librarians should create electronic databases of their digitised information packages for timely storage, retrieval and reuse.

- *Individual-centric*: Some information packaging is derived from individual user needs or requests. For example, an instructor might work with the subject reference librarian to develop an online course reader. The library might integrate an RSS feed option for their online catalogue to inform users of new titles. A librarian might research technology literacy requirements in other institutions, and write a white paper for an academic policies committee. Individual-centric packaging is usually produced on demand – which may be immediate or planned well in advance. Technology, particularly telecommunications, speeds the flow of information – and user expectations.

- *Program-centric*: In general, curriculum programmes drive higher education. They represent the focus of the institution – and the teaching faculty therein. Because most programmes seek stability and longevity, information packaging for programmes can be incorporated into long-term planning – as well as done in response to short-term needs. As librarians keep up-to-date about academic changes or curricular modifications, they can develop information packages to frontload their services in support of those initiatives. In a few cases, programmes collaborate to support resource allocations, but usually each programme is only focused on its own information needs. Subject librarians can increase their credibility and value as they work with specific programmes to develop useful information packages such as bibliographies, discipline-based research strategy guidelines, collections of data sets, repositories of learning objects, and syntheses of current research efforts. On the other hand, because reference librarians tend to work across curricular areas, they can modify existing information packages to serve several programmes' needs; for instance, a bibliography for the philosophy programme might be slightly modified for a history programme. Technology can further facilitate communication among librarians, and between librarians and teaching faculty, to provide timely and focused information packages.

- *Services-centric*: Academic support services are sometimes overlooked in information packaging initiatives, yet hold great potential for bringing together disparate parts of the campus. For instance, an international students service may need to identify local entities that could help their clientele; academic librarians can help them create local referral databases. A gay/lesbian/bisexual/transgender centre may want to collect and disseminate information about relevant campus resources; academic librarians can provide bibliographies and also help the centre staff organise identified items into an accessible database. Health services might observe risky student behaviour, and want to provide information as a preventative measure; librarians can help package and disseminate such information. Services for students with special needs can help library technical staff make sure that all information packages are universally accessible.

Format

As reference librarians create information packages, one of the main considerations nowadays is format: what is the most effective and efficient way to represent packaged information? Representative reference products include, by format:

- *print*: bibliographies, library orientations, facilities maps, library periodicals, research guides and handbooks, institutional history monographs;
- *video*: library orientations, information literacy instruction, institutional documentaries;
- *audio*: library orientations, information literacy instruction, institutional interviews and presentations;
- *optical disc*: library orientations, reference-related databases, information literacy instruction, research guides and handbooks, institutional interviews and presentations, collections of library-related images;
- *web-based*: library orientations, facilities maps, bibliographies and other library reference databases, library periodicals, information

literacy instruction, research guides and handbooks, institutional documents.

Each format has its advantages and disadvantages. For instance, print documents can be quickly produced and modified, and they are easy to handle. However, printing and distribution costs for long, professional-looking documents can be prohibitive. Audio and video provide non-textual information, and reflect today's growing multimedia sensibilities, but they require specialised production and editing equipment, and might not be accessible by users with special needs. Optical disc storage can accommodate large files and can be cheap to duplicate, but they too require hardware and software to develop and use. The Internet offers an additional feature that is hard to duplicate in any other form: open-ended interactivity. Web tutorials, for instance, can keep track of user behaviours and can link to resources beyond the tutorial itself. Static products can be complemented with ongoing service, such as 24/7 online reference service. While service is not a packaged product per se, the *structure* of the reference service (e.g. online real-time chat) is, in a sense, a packaging of information.

Digitisation efforts

Many academic libraries are involved in digitisation projects, mainly to preserve and make accessible unique documents such as local history or rare primary sources, some of which can serve as reference tools. This process requires specialised equipment and expertise, which are sometimes outsourced. Outside funding for these initiatives is generally pursued from consortia, foundations and government entities. Typically, with outside funding comes a stipulation that outside entities can access the materials electronically. However, knowledge about and access to these collections can be patchy.

The processing of such collections can also be uneven. For instance, the Library of Congress has 16 digital collections, each with its own unique cataloguing procedures, the result of customising the database to serve the unique research needs of its specialised clientele. While a 'shell' search engine provides access to each collection separately or collectively, the results of the search can be unpredictable because no consistent authority control or other metatagging standard exists.

Nevertheless, the most important issue in digitisation is not technical but managerial. As with other collections, academic librarians need to how long to store, organise and provide access to digitised materials; associated digital policies need to align with existing collection policies and take into consideration the verities of technology. Unfortunately, most institutions do not have the expertise and equipment to control digitising projects independently, so they have to enter into agreements with other entities, which requires careful and trustworthy negotiations.

Legal issues

Several legal issues loom when dealing with technology aspects of library-packaged information:

- *Content*: Does the library have permission to copy, download, digitise, modify, excerpt or package information? What limitations exist on such practices, e.g. length of time to keep the copy, number of copies (sometimes within a specified timeframe), extent of copying (such as percentage of the entire work), access rights, purpose limitations (such as referral vs. personal research vs. resale), format.

- *Format*: Packaging information, such as software installation instructions, for internal use, is a much different issue than scanning published cartoons for a public website. Even if the library gets permission to copy an image, that permission might not extend to resizing or cropping the image. Copyright owners might not permit content to be reformatted or repurposed with reason, as changing context can result in different interpretations of the information. Likewise, pinning up candid student pictures in the library mailroom requires a different level of permission than broadcasting those same pictures on the Internet, particularly if any under-age students are shown. Indeed, because of stalking and other criminal behaviours, few libraries show captioned pictures of their staff, particularly in online environments.

- *Liability*: Libraries need to read licensing agreements carefully to make sure that their packaging efforts comply with the legal language. Users need equitable access, proper authorisation, and confidentiality; moreover, no profits can be incurred (Farb and Riggio, 2004). Once librarians start to extract and synthesise information, even with permission, they risk being sued. For instance, a user who follows health information might suffer unpleasant results. Especially in the areas of law and health, librarians need to make sure that they post a disclaimer that they are not legal or health professionals (unless so licensed). Even the software used to package information is likely to entail legal right for its use, particularly if the product is web-based and disseminated externally. The North Carolina State Library Web Portal Collection Development Policy (*http://www.ncecho.org/colldev .asp*) addresses a number of these issues.

Development

At the most basic level, developing technology-enhanced information packages includes four competencies: assessment skills (ability to identify needs, audiences, information), content knowledge (the information to be packaged), communication skill (how to organise and present the information), and media skill (how to select an appropriate format and present information in that communications medium). Technological expertise is usually linked with the media aspect of information packaging.

An individual may possess all of these competencies, and proceed to package information independently. Typically, such efforts have a short-term timeframe and use pattern. As needs, information and technology become more complex, reference librarians need to collaborate in developing larger-scale information packages. Particularly within a large institution, no one person knows all the curricula, all the information sources, or all the technology options; indeed, any person trying to master all those skill sets would probably become very overwhelmed. Instead, reference librarians need to know their peers' competencies so they can complement one another's contributions. Additionally, they need to be able to access and share their efforts to reduce duplicative efforts and optimise information package repurposing.

Ideally, information packaging should constitute part of the overall reference and information services programme. As such, reference librarians should collaborate with the rest of the academic community in order to map the curriculum, aligning it with information literacy standards. Based on systematic assessment of needs, they can then ascertain what information needs to be packaged – and how. Indeed, entire library enterprises could package information collectively for the good of the entire system.

Another model centres on the teaching faculty who want to share their knowledge, be it in research or in instruction. Learning modules, data sets, white papers, and even student work can be deposited into a central server – or the metadata for these documents can be stored centrally. In this scenario, librarians provide the organisational structure, particularly in cataloguing the documents. A database administrator also needs to be part of the planning team in order to program and maintain the technical part of the database (Patrizio, 2006). Librarians can also make good use of such repositories by harvesting the data therein to align items with information literacy standards.

One of the major obstacles to collaborative information packaging efforts is electronic interoperability. Examples of collaboratively-developed technology-enhanced information packaging structures follow:

- *Open Directory Project (DMOZ)*: Essentially an open source set of web directories, DMOZ depends on volunteer contributors and editors. Within the project, the Association of Research Libraries maintains a directory of electronic journals, newsletters and academic discussion lists (*http://dsej.arl.org*). Florida International University focuses on information literacy efforts in academic libraries (*http://www.fiu.edu/~library/ili*). The Center for Research and Development of Digital Libraries, based at the University of North Carolina, collaborates with other academic institutions to provide information about digital library development and management (*http://ils.unc.edu/cradle*).

- *DSpace*: Developed by MIT and Hewlett-Packard, this open source archive solution is used by over 140 institutions and reflects a management system that is structured for a university system. Input privileges can extend to department level to enable broad-based contributions. The back-end programming and customisation needed may limit its use to technology-savvy institutions (*http://www.dspace .org*).

- *Open Content Alliance* (OCA): This collaborative international initiative, which involves academic institutions among other entities, seeks to build a searchable digital archive of multilingual texts and multimedia resources (*http://www.opencontentalliance.org*). A similar open source project, LOCKSS (Lots of Copies Keep Stuff Safe) is a free software program that enables libraries to 'collect, store, preserve, and provide access to their own, local copy of authorised content they purchase' (*http://www.lockss.org*).

- *Sakai Project*: Several universities are collaboratively developing course management tools that can interface with digital repositories (*http://www.sakaiproject.org*).

Even though technology enables such projects to develop, the main impetus – and potential obstacle – is the practice of submitting material to the database. Faculty have to see the benefit of sharing their labour-intensive efforts: for instruction, for research, for service – and for retention and promotion.

Dissemination

Just because reference libraries package information does not mean that those products will be used by the academic community. As an established entity, reference and information services need to be considered as valuable, affordable and accessible. Close communication and collaboration are needed between the library staff and the rest of the institution. Librarians need to plan how to disseminate and market such packages. In terms of timing, information packages can be disseminated on a just-in-time basis or on a regular schedule. In terms of format, librarians need to align content and targeted audience so that the information will be physically and intellectually accessible. Librarians should also identify existing dissemination channels in order to build on existing high-profile structures so that they do not have to expend extra effort in making people aware of the medium as well as the message; it should be noted that the most effective communications channel may well be word-of-mouth. Whenever possible, reference librarians should develop and disseminate information packages in collaboration with, and in support of, other academic community stakeholders.

The Reference and User Services Association (RUSA) of the American Library Association (ALA) recommends the following actions, which all emphasise human expertise and professional relationships.

- Build psychological bonds through user focus, courtesy, speedy response, competence, and professionalism.
- Build value bonds through focus on excellence, proactive innovation, and mass customisation.
- Build bonds through structure: frontline information systems, user-oriented processes, and compensation based on user satisfaction (Sheth, 2002).

Types of technology-enhanced information packages

Reference librarians create a variety of information packages in alignment with the mission of the academic community, and sometimes with the help of their academic peers.

CAS/SDI

Although academic librarians are consulted by academic researchers mainly at 'sticking points' when the academic community cannot find specific needed information, when reference librarians set up user research interest profiles, they can provide a current awareness service (CAS) or selective dissemination of information (SDI) manually via e-mail, listservs, user groups, blogs and ongoing webliographies. Alternatively, they can incorporate – and teach users how to take advantage of – automated systems to deliver timely periodical content services, book alerting services, aggregating services, RSS feeds and other electronic services.

These services can provide great just-in-time information, but they require technical expertise in setting them up and strong marketing efforts so that the academic community will be aware of their existence and use them. Before investing the requisite technological effort to modify existing systems to incorporate CAS, librarians should meet with academic community stakeholders to determine the potential need and interest in this service. In the meantime, subject librarians should get to know their teaching faculty counterparts so they can become aware of instructional and research interests. In that respect, developing and implementing an online survey to obtain faculty information profiles is a good first step in establishing CAS. York University's survey represents a low-key effort in this direction (Fernandez, 2002).

Linking sources

The naïve user would like a single-stop searching tool linking all relevant material: primary sources, secondary sources, print, web-based, audiovisual. Being able to discern the relationship between those sources would add another dimension of scholarship. The new Functional Requirements of Bibliographic Records conceptual model offers a method to link sources, using the power of technology to support users' searches. This model also reveals the difficulty that librarians may encounter in trying to establish these relationships systematically, particularly in light of existing library catalogues. While a one-stop tool is probably not feasible in the near future (despite Google's intention), smaller-scale reference linking has become an attractive way to add value to information, and facilitate integrated reference and information services.

Links may be categorised as either static (created as a permanent link) or dynamic (created in response to user action). Normally, libraries pursue dynamic solutions where linking can occur without full control of the resources. This approach is attractive – in theory – to libraries, but may threaten vendors who are less comfortable about open access. Furthermore, as librarians create documents that include links, be it at the citation or source level, they need to consider how the source information is captured and authenticated, processing between links, and hosting services. All entities and related protocols need to be interoperable as well as legally compliant (Van de Sompel and Hochstenbach, 1999).

There are several ways to link reference sources:

- between citations (e.g. databases);
- within sources (e.g. hyperlinks);
- between sources and applications (e.g. course management systems);
- between sources and services (e.g. e-reserves).

Usually, metadata provides the basis for these actions. Digital object identifiers (DOIs) provide an international standards-based 'system for persistent and actionable identification and interoperable exchange of managed information on digital networks' (*http://www.doi.org*). The underlying premise is that resources might be used by individuals beyond the technical control of the original describer. Scripting enables records to be related, and mark-up language enables data to be transferred online. Linking software, such as SFX, act as middleware between reference services, drilling down to the level of individual records.

Reference librarians can make good use of reference linking in several ways. The most common packaged product is a library web portal that links sources through research guides. An extension of this effort is course management systems, whereby identified reference resources can be linked to academic programmes and specific courses; subject specialist librarians can provide valuable expertise to teaching faculty when they have the opportunity to help create supporting reference lists. Linking resources in response to varying degrees of information needed, librarian-created information literacy web tutorials can include hyperlinks to relevant supportive details, enabling users to self-determine the depth of information needed to conduct research.

Repositories

Increasingly, reference libraries are developing digital repositories, either storing data or storing the documents themselves. In both cases, these services manage and disseminate digital resources. The scope of repositories can range from a single programme to international consortia. Key goals of a repository – and their technological implications follow:

- maintaining the data without damage or alteration: storage and security requirements;

- providing 'physical' access to the data, including extracting it from the archive: authentification, verification, identification, metadata harvesting software;

- ensuring that the user can understand and interpret the data: display/rendering software and preservation planning;

- ensuring long-term stability: technology planning and data maintenance (Wheatley, 2004).

The value of repositories lies in the quality of use of their content, so identifying desired kinds of documents and collecting high-quality materials are key functions. Possible content may range from learning objects to major works, and may reflect existing resources or serve as a motivator for creating applicable items. As the idea of repositories is explored, all stakeholders need to provide input into its development and implementation. In some cases, information literacy might be the focus so that academic librarians could take an instructional lead, but in most cases, reference repositories need to develop in response to academic discipline needs. Other roles for reference librarians relative to institutional repositories include project planning and management, collection definition, understanding software, metadata guidance, submission review and author training (Allard, Mack, and Feitner-Reichert, 2005).

In structuring repositories, librarians need to consider three layers: storage, database and application. While librarians are good organisers, all of these layers will entail technological expertise, so librarians need to communicate clearly with their technological colleagues to ensure ease of use for the academic community. The Association and Research Libraries of the American Library Association developed an institutional repository SPEC toolkit to help librarians with policies and procedures (*http://www.arl.org/spec/SPEC292web.pdf*).

One promising practice in digitising reference materials is systemwide technology initiatives, usually in the form of federated repositories of archival materials. DSpace (*http://www.dspace.org*) is an Open Archive Initiative that provides guidelines for digitising, cataloguing, storing and disseminating unique digital sources. This open source solution emphasises the need for technical expertise and planning.

Even before installing the software, DSpace recommends that the following considerations be discussed and resolved:

- determining how each campus will use it, what content will be collected, and who can contribute;
- determining what role the library will play in planning and implementation;
- marketing DSpace to the academic community;
- testing the product on a small scale before fully deploying it.

Other examples of open source repository software mentioned by Wheatley (2004) include:

- ARNO (*http://www.uba.uva.nl/arno*): Dutch-based document storage and metadata database;
- CDS Invenio (*http://cdsware.cern.ch/invenio/index.html*): integrated digital library system developed by CERN;
- Eprints (*http://www.eprints.org/software*): British software developed in PERL with a MySQL database layer;
- FEDORA (*http://www.fedora.info*): Java-based repository and digital library system that associates web services and objects;
- MyCoRe (*http://www.mycore.de/*): built by several German universities, this Java-script program allows use of different database back-ends.

Knowledge management

Knowledge management (KM) basically consists of managing the knowledge of an organisation, usually collecting, storing, organising and disseminating explicit information such as documents, with the intent that others will use that information. Usually, the intent of knowledge management is staff productivity: gathering information about the flow of information, identifying possible sources of information, and empowering administrators. The need for knowledge management increases as employees gain specialised expertise and the system as a whole exceeds its ability to communicate individual knowledge easily. Particularly in today's society where in-house knowledge may be proprietary and employees may leave after a short time, making tacit knowledge explicit through the use of a knowledge management system offers an effective way to coalesce expertise.

As might be expected, knowledge management systems usually consist of a searchable database of digital information. A technical and governance infrastructure needs to be in place for KM efforts to succeed. Some of the issues that have to be addressed include:

- the goal of the KM effort;
- metadata standards for each contributed item;
- software to support the database;
- quality control of the sources – and their processing;
- incentives for contributing;
- support (technical, financial, administrative) (Farmer, 2005).

Reference librarians might use knowledge management systems in a couple of ways: (1) to cross-fertilise expertise within the library, across a multi-campus system, or across different library systems; (2) to help the academic community incorporate information literacy effectively across the curriculum; (3) to facilitate professional development. As with other instances of repositories, KM value is derived from the content therein, so members of the enterprise have to see the value of sharing their hard-earned knowledge. An investment model can serve as an analogy: as each person contributes to the collective body of knowledge, each person receives the wisdom of the rest of the enterprise. Markus (2001) suggests that different types of users might approach KM in unique ways. Novice users would be looking for expertise, such as entering librarians or teaching faculty. Shared work practitioners would locate and repurpose other people's contributions. Shared work producers would identify knowledge gaps and create needed documents. Secondary knowledge miners outside the environment would seek ideas to enrich their own domain.

UNESCO Bangkok has developed a promising knowledge management repository (*http://www.unescobkk.org/index.php?id=1932*), which they label as an e-library, with the intent of providing policy and programme information for Asia-Pacific countries. It serves both the in-house needs of UNESCO offices as well as serving as an outreach initiative to inform the general public.

E-publishing

For decades, in order to inform their constituents, reference librarians have created documents for their institutions, their professional colleagues, and for the public. These might be as simple as a guide to the library or as exhaustive as the history of an entire institution. A few academic libraries have also published journals, such as the University of Illinois's *Library Trends* and Clarion University of Pennsylvania's *Rural Libraries*. In the digital world, reference librarians are exploring the benefits – and challenges of – scholarly e-publishing. For example:

- Stanford University Library's HighWire Press, which publishes almost 1,000 e-journals. The press prides itself in its efforts to incorporate multimedia, hyperlinks, interactivity and powerful search engines.

- Parallel Press, directed by the University of Wisconsin-Madison, publishes on-demand books that parallel print times and chapbooks about local poets and historians.

- The E-Press has operated as a separate department within the Swedish Linköping University Library since 2004. It publishes digital conference proceedings, databases, journals, series, theses and reports. The press states that it will maintain availability of its publications for 25 years, and that its authors retain individual copyrights.

In a few cases, one of the impetuses is financial gain, but for the majority of library e-publishers the goal is dissemination of information on topics of interest to academics. To this end, open access journals have become quite attractive: they are relatively inexpensive to create (except for labour costs of editing and layout) and disseminate, can include digital features not available in print format such as sound, and may be more timely to publish than print versions. The Budapest Open Access Initiative (2002) asserts that

> Removing access barriers to this literature will accelerate research, enrich education, share the learning of the rich with the poor and the poor with the rich, make this literature as useful as it can be, and lay the foundation for uniting humanity in a common intellectual conversation and quest for knowledge.

On the other hand, maintaining a permanent collection of the e-publications may be overlooked. Furthermore, if indexing services do not receive a copy of the journal, then access to the information will become even more limited. The best guide to scholarly e-publishing is Bailey's *Open access bibliography: Liberating scholarly literature with e-prints and open access journals* (*http://www.digital-scholarship.com/oab/oab.htm*).

As with other packaging efforts, e-publishing requires a clear imperative and objective. Stakeholders have to determine the scope, frequency, target audience and dissemination plan. The library also needs to allocate sufficient material and human resources to support such endeavours. Usually only libraries with well-established publishing experience venture into the cyberprint world. Chan, Kwok and Yip (2005) list steps that librarians should address when starting e-publication efforts:

1. Evaluate the technical software in terms of technical requirements, interface, database structure, search options, reliability, support, export options.

2. Create and interpret policies on selection, copyright, indexing, format and archiving.

3. Solicit and build content: conference papers, reports, research, working papers, websites.

4. Liaison with the academic community: educate, advocate, advise.

5. Provide reference assistance in using new e-publications.

The creative commons

A growing interest in the creative 'information commons' reflects a philosophy that 'information yearns to be free' and that accessible information leads to expanded discourse, knowledge and progress. Public domain documents have exemplified this philosophy for over a century, and government publications carry on this tradition in the spirit of civic engagement. The basic premise in using the creative commons is that individuals can access and use the materials freely, but they have to credit the originator, and they should share any modifications of the information with the creative commons community. In 2005, the International Federation of Library Associations and Institutions (IFLA) called upon the World Summit on the Information Society Summit to promote a global information commons where all people could access and disseminate information without restrictions (Byrne, 2005).

Two main approaches to the creative commons have emerged: (1) contributing and modifying original information, and (2) facilitating the *sharing* of information. The latter function most closely approximates core library philosophy. Union catalogues and other collective databases exemplify how materials can be made known to outside entities. Interlibrary loan protocols provide equitable service for sharing resources, with state or national governmental entities supporting those interactions financially.

The Internet has become the de facto communications vehicle for sharing documents in the twenty-first century. A federated approach to digital resource sharing mirrors traditional practices. While one server may collect all the metadata about relevant information – a centralised operation, the actual information is stored in many locations – a decentralised operation. In some cases, access is limited to members of the participating libraries (the typical case for subscription databases) but in other instances, access is open to any person (such as repositories of learning objects). The main difference between old union catalogues and emerging collective databases is that the process has collapsed from a two-step operation (i.e. locating the item and then requesting it) to one: accessing the information directly through a linked database.

At the local level, individual institutions may use local area network servers and intranets to share information. Some course management systems, such as BeachBoard, offer a means to store materials for retrieval by the entire academic community. Learning objects, modular content or learning activities that focus on a specific concept, have particular appeal because they can be used in several courses or even across disciplines. With their expertise in organisation and connections with technical help, librarians are uniquely positioned to organise these learning object collections or at least provide a structure for metatagging the items to optimise retrieval. Librarians can also contribute their own learning objects, usually pertaining to information literacy, for access and integration by teaching faculty across the campus. However, as with other library resources, these objects need to be publicised and explained in order to optimise use.

The idea of a creative commons can be expanded across systems, disciplines, even national boundaries. Examples of federated repositories include:

- Open Video Project (*http://ww.open-video.org*);
- MERLOT (*http://www.merlot.org*) and its European counterpart ARIADNE (*www.ariadne-eu.org*);
- DSpace (*http://www.dspace.org*);
- Net Academy Universe (*http://www.netacademy.org*);
- Digital Library of the Commons (*http://dlc.dlib.indiana.edu*);
- Open Directory Project (ODP) (*http://dmoz.org/about.html*);
- UK National Archive (*http://www.nationalarchives.gov.uk/*);
- European Library (*http://theeuropeanlibrary.org*);
- ArchiveGrid (*http://www.archivegrid.org*);
- Global Memory Net (*www.memorynet.org/*);
- China Digital Museum Project (*http://wiki.dspace.org/ ChinaDigitalMuseumProject*).

Oliver and Swain (2006) listed a variety of international digital repositories, noting each one's record structure. They recommended the University of Nottingham's model, OpenDOAR (*http://www.opendoar .org*) because of its easy retrieval and updating mechanisms.

Libraries are also embracing the creative commons arena of electronic journals. Particularly as the academic community pursues research venues, providing efficient access to e-journals is a logical function for academic libraries. The Scholarly Publishing and Academic Resources Coalition (SPARC) (*http://www.arl.org/sparc*), founded in 1998, exemplifies a collaborative library approach to disseminating research. Because of such open interchanges, more citations have been included in studies, and scientific advances have been accelerated (Lawrence, 2001). The following sites represent e-journal depository collaboration, some of which are discipline-specific:

- BioOne (*http://www.bioone.org*);

- New England Law Library Consortium Legal Scholarship Repository (*http://lsr.nellco.org*);

- eScholarship Repository (*http://repositories.cdlib.org/escholarship*);

- Digital Academic Repository of the University of Amsterdam (*http://dare.uva.nl/en*);

- Érudit (*www.erudit.org*);

- Oxford Text Archive (*http://ota.ahds.ac.uk*).

One of the advantages of federated collaborations is that each site typically controls copyright and licensing issues. Nevertheless, these consortia initiatives require careful, thorough planning, not only in terms of technical requirements but also in terms of fiscal and governance issues. Because metadata comprise a core element in these repositories, all stakeholders have to agree on database fields, controlled vocabulary, technical standards, document exchange format, process protocols, storage issues and security.

5

Technology impact on physical access to reference and information services

Tracey Mayfield

Imagine this: A student sits at a desk in his darkened dorm room. It is very late and the dorms are unusually quiet. The only light comes from his laptop and a small desk lamp. The student sits hunched over his computer and looks distressed. He has an 8–10-page research paper to do, and he has waited until the last minute. His professor has told him that he needs to use the library's resources to find scholarly research articles, and he cannot use Google. He has no idea how to do complete this assignment.

He starts at the library's homepage. On the main library web page, he sees a section on doing research and finding articles. He finds his way to the research databases page and finds a database that looks like it would help on his topic. He begins to search. After some trial and error, he finds a list of results that yields ten full-text articles, which is what he needs for his reference list.

He writes his paper in the dim light, referring to the ten articles he has found in the database. He sighs heavily when he types his last line and reads the professor's instructions again. He yelps when he reads that the paper needs to be formatted according to the APA guidelines. He goes back to the library's website and finds a section on citation styles. He is able to format the paper using the examples on the library's website. He prints out the final version of the paper, smiles and turns out the light to catch what little sleep he can before his first class. The student conducted his research, wrote his paper and correctly formatted the paper all without ever setting foot in the library.

Now imagine this: A student has to begin preparing her thesis for her master's degree. She has written many papers throughout her college career, but is uncomfortable with a project of this size and is very nervous about the task that lies ahead of her. Her thesis advisor suggests she contact the librarian assigned to her discipline. The student sends the librarian an e-mail asking for help. The librarian arranges to meet with the student in the librarian's office.

When the student arrives for the appointment, she is nervous and anxious. The librarian is friendly and sympathetic and spends an hour with the student guiding and giving her direction on where she needs to start her research. She guides the student through library catalogue and database searches, shows the student software that will help her organise her citations and help with her bibliography. She shows the student how to request items through interlibrary loan. The student, very grateful and relieved, leaves the librarian's office to go use the library's computing commons to start the research. Over the next few months, the student is a familiar face in the library, using the library's computers and collections and occasionally stopping by the reference desk to ask a question or two.

Lastly, imagine this: A student with a mobility disability who requires a wheelchair enters the library. She needs to do some research for her portion of a group project for a class. She decides to visit the library while up on the side of campus where the library is located. The student enters the reference area where a large group of computers is bustling with students hard at work doing research and checking e-mail. The student sees a clearly marked sign above a computer indicating that the machine is equipped with an electronic screen reader and electronic zoom text software; the table that holds all this equipment is an electronic table that is height-adjustable. The student is able to sit comfortably at a computer and do her research, and she is able to find all the resources she needs to complete her section of the group project. She also takes advantage of the computer to check her e-mail, and she is able to do all this with her dignity intact, without feeling as though she is calling special attention to herself.

However, during the course of the student's research, she finds several books that she needs. The student goes to the reference librarian to ask for help in retrieving two of the books she needs. The books she needs are located too high on the shelves for her to reach in her wheelchair and therefore she cannot get them by herself. The reference librarian, who is very friendly and helpful, accompanies the student to the book stacks and helps retrieve the books that are out of the student's reach. The student is able to check the books out and leaves the library generally content, but a bit unhappy that she needed to ask for help.

In the three scenarios described above, did technology hinder any of the student's experiences with the library? Did the thesis student who physically accessed the library have a 'better' experience than the student who was able to accomplish his research via their home computer? All of the students completed their research and fulfilled the requirements of their projects/assignments 'via' the library, but the human element (or lack thereof), and how that affects their quality of experience is where the questions might arise. So much of what librarians do to provide reference and information services can be dependent on in-depth, in-person and personal interactions; and if so many of the services are available off-site, remotely and online, how does that affect what they do as human services professionals? Can the elements of technology, reference and information services and human interaction peacefully coexist? Are they mutually exclusive? How do other factors such as library facilities, course management systems, resource sharing, and library portals figure into the equation? How these three concepts all relate, affect each other, and intersect will be discussed in this chapter.

Technology, libraries and service, oh my!

Technology is omnipresent in academic libraries today. Even the hardcore Luddites, eagerly awaiting the rebirth of the card catalogue would agree that technology is pervasive in a library. Online catalogues have replaced card catalogues, electronic databases have (largely) replaced print indexes, various methods of online tutorials are meant to replace some library instruction, and most services are outlined on a library's website instead of paper flyers and handouts. Course management systems (CMS) are allowing professors and librarians to hold class sessions and discussions 'virtually'. Software programs build citations and bibliographies, renew books from off-campus, and tell students to get off the computer when their time is up. In some libraries, controversy has erupted over computers taking over space previously occupied by book stacks (Carlson, 2006). In other libraries, scandals brew over students clamouring for space to study in groups, violating the long held tradition for a quiet, tomb-like atmosphere they expect in a library (DiMattia, 2005). There is really no aspect of librarianship that has not been touched by technology.

Reference and information services have had to change with the technological times. Reference librarians are asked a myriad of questions today in an ever-changing reference environment. In addition to receiving questions about 'where the restrooms are', 'where is this particular book', and 'how do I find an article', they are asked to aid students adding classes to their schedules online, as well as explain how particular functions work in Microsoft Word and Excel. They are asked questions about using CMS for student classwork, and they are asked how to add money to their student accounts. They are asked by faculty about copyright infringement issues in adding full-text articles to electronic reserves and how to use plagiarism software programs. In short, they are asked questions that have nothing to do with what would be considered traditional reference and everything to do with technology.

How does this ever-changing technological reference and information service environment affect the human element to the services we provide? Does it help or hinder? Does it affect it at all? To answer these questions, there are several factors that affect this delicate balance of technology, reference and information services and the human element that should be examined.

Library facilities

There is much discussion in the library literature about the library as 'place'. The allocation of physical space in a library can be a hot commodity and just as controversial as the materials inside of it. Some feel that academic libraries should still mainly exist as book and print material repositories (Weise, 2004). Others feel exactly opposite: that books and print materials are passé and that the modern academic library should provide space for students to gather, socialise and study, while providing all research materials electronically (Weise, 2004). Yet others feel that a balance can be struck between the first two scenarios and provide the best of both worlds; a place where students feel comfortable socialising and studying, while providing a solid collection of online and print materials for research (Weise, 2004). All these opinions point to one unwavering fact: that online and networked services have radically changed the popular conception of information environments (Savolainen, 2006).

When discussing the human aspect of library services, the physical layout of the building itself can be a point of contention. Before the ubiquitous availability of computers in libraries, patrons were greeted by a person when they entered a library. In most libraries, this is still the case. Patrons are greeted by a circulation desk, a reference desk, an information kiosk, or some sort of personal greeting in addition to computers. Does it really matter whom or what greets patrons when they enter the building? From a service perspective, the answer is: absolutely.

Physical organisation in a library is not the only form of organisation that bears exploration into the discussion of technology and information services. Other forms of organisation, such as the organisation and standardisation of services in both technical and public services domains, deserve attention and examination as an element in the overall facilities and services discussion.

Technology in technical services has advanced steadily over the years, but the automation and standardisation of public services has taken a different path (Kleiner, 1993). While access services have adapted easily to fairly standardised automation systems, the human element of reference services, with no viable way to standardise or automate the in-person interaction, has not followed suit (Kleiner, 1993). In addition, those reference services that have given way to automation, such as electronic databases for article searching, do not subscribe to any standard format. Although most electronic databases provide similar information (e.g. citations, Boolean capabilities), hardware, software, and platforms vary considerably. Therefore, reference and information services librarians must practise constant vigilance to stay up-to-date with all the different online tools. They must then be sufficiently comfortable with these tools to communicate and teach this disorganised schema to the uninitiated user. This lack of standardisation seems to grow with each new technological innovation. The difference in database interfaces poses a challenge to the user in terms of functionality and usability. With the rise in popularity of full-text articles, more guidance is required in how exactly to retrieve them (either via the database, open access, or link resolver services such as SFX).

When discussing technology and reference and information services, it is imperative to consider the needs of disabled patrons. When it comes to physical space, it is understood that US libraries need to comply with the Americans with Disabilities Act 1990; however, libraries also need to be compliant online. Technology allows autonomy, but if librarians do not work to make their online resources compliant and accessible, they are providing a disservice to a large portion of the academic community.

The first step in making online resources inclusive to disabled patrons is to understand the range of disabilities that patrons have and their needs for access. This can be accomplished by working in close cooperation with a the campus disabled students services centre. This office can provide a wealth of information about the academic disabled community that will assist the library in providing tools to make resources accessible. Minor adjustments to existing services have a huge impact on these patrons. Making sure the library's website is compliant and accessible, adding a few text enlargers and screen reading software, as well as height adjustable tables can allow for access to all. If space permits, not shelving print materials on the utmost upper and lower shelves in book stacks, and allowing extra width in the spacing of book stack shelving allows for accessibility and comfort for all (Lodge, 2004). Indeed, a mindset of universal design should frame reference service in general.

Library web portals

If a goal of academic librarians is to provide personal access and services to the academic community (Weise, 2004), then a library web portal is the gateway to accomplishing that goal. A library web portal is described as 'a user-driven, customisable interface to collections of Internet resources' (Morgan, 2005), or as 'a single user interface for access to a wide variety of electronic resources both within and outside of the library' (Boss, 2005). Web portals tend to provide the following service components (Boss, 2005):

- intuitive and customisable web interface;
- personalised content presentation;
- federated searching;
- relevancy ranking;
- link resolution;
- security;
- communications and collaboration.

Each of these service components strives to meet the needs of patrons by providing customised services that they can access online. Boss (2005) notes that just using the federated searching component does not constitute a web portal; rather, all or most of the components listed above need to be utilised to be considered a web portal.

So how do web portals affect reference and information services? Like many other services the library provides, instruction and guidance are needed to demonstrate to library patrons that the web portal exists, and to show how to take advantage of it. One of the disadvantages of a web portal (and especially federated searching) can be retrieving too many results from a single search (Boss, 2005; Crawford, 2002). Patrons need to understand the concepts behind this tool so that they can effectively search independently.

Course management systems

Course management systems (CMS) are another type of technological learning tool that can and should be considered as another means for academic librarians to become more involved in the learning and teaching mission of the larger institution. One of the biggest problems with CMS, however, has been the lack of library involvement or even a mention of libraries in the planning and creation of most CMS tools (*Library Technology Reports*, 2005). Therefore, most enterprising librarians have inserted themselves into the process to learn about CMS and how they are being used on campus in order to provide much-needed input.

However, no level of self-initiative can completely bridge the technological gap that exists between CMS and library services. Currently, it is difficult to integrate library services into CMS. In some cases, a button is available to link to the library's website; however, any in-depth searching and article retrieval from the CMS is not currently possible. Students and faculty must link out of the CMS and into the library's web pages to then be authenticated in order to use the library's databases and online tools. This does not bode well for today's Millennial/NetGen student and their expectation of seamless online searching capability (*Library Technology Reports*, 2005).

What implications does this have for the library's reference services? Academic librarians need to learn yet another technological tool that they, in turn, will need to teach to their patrons. While in most cases, the library is not technically a part of the CMS (organisationally or otherwise), librarians field questions from both faculty and students about the usage and protocol of the CMS, and will need to be educated enough to answer intelligently. As a future goal, library integration (and librarian input) in CMS would be ideal, but it will take monumental effort on the part of libraries to show CMS producers and creators that librarians and libraries are a necessary part of this technology (*Library Technology Reports*, 2005). It will probably take a collective effort on the part of library consortia and organisations to offer enough leverage to influence these service providers.

Resource sharing

What impact does resource sharing and consortial buying have on physical access to reference and information services? Plenty. In fact, consortial buying and sharing of resources is fast becoming commonplace. In addition to augmenting an individual library's collection, consortia allow for more negotiation in the costs of materials (Borek et al., 2006). When a patron needs a book that is unavailable in their home library or already checked out, it can often be requested seamlessly from a member of the consortium. Research databases that would normally be out of the price range for a small library can be purchased via consortial agreement. Leverage can be used to work around the skyrocketing costs of scholarly journals and electronic databases by the collective purchasing power of a consortium.

While possibly a 'selfish' motive for working together, the consortia partnership is positive. No matter what the consortial scenario, or motive behind the partnership, the patron wins. They have seamless access to many more materials at no additional cost, while the partnering libraries take advantage of the shared collections to serve them better. With minimal instruction on requesting items via the library's interlibrary services, they have many more resources at their fingertips (Borek et al., 2006).

Global implications

In the end, academic libraries are service providers. Today's academic library should and will continue to be a service organisation that contributes to and supports the mission of the university it serves (Weise, 2004). *How* library staff provide service is constantly changing, but as long as the necessary services are provided and as long as the patrons served are happy and getting what they need, everyone wins.

The current literature concludes that most library patrons use a combination of electronic and in-person processes when utilising the library's information resources and services (Bejune and Kinkus, 2006). In revisiting the three scenarios from the beginning of this chapter, all patrons were served. All three were able to accomplish their research and complete their assignments and projects. All were able to reach their goals by using the library. Whether or not they interacted with a person or simply made use of the electronic resources, they used the library's services and had successful interactions with the library.

As anyone who has had problems using online software or programs (and their sometimes-helpful Help functions), technology cannot ever replace the 'hand holding' and personal attention that a reference and information services professional provides, and to assume any differently is 'customer disservice' (Jassin, 2005). It really does seem as though the more online services the library offers, the more that are needed.

To be pragmatic about the resolution, the academic community wants the ease and accessibility of online access *and* the human contact and interaction that only librarians can provide (Weise, 2004). What academic librarians as information professionals need to be doing is ensuring that the physical buildings, the online and in-person services, and the print and electronic resources meet all of these needs to the best of their abilities. Librarians will never be able to perfectly predict in what form the academic community will need or want reference services – in person, in print or online. However, a focused and multi-faceted strategy for meeting patron needs, will allow academic librarians to be there for them, in whatever form they desire.

6

Technology impact on intellectual access for reference and information services

Tiffini Travis and Lesley Farmer

A student is having trouble finding different cultures' perceptions of aging, and asks the reference librarian for help. Books do not seem to cover the topic, so the librarian suggests dissertations and articles. He then guides the student in combining appropriate keywords, and shows how to use wildcards to expand the number of possible resources. The librarian also shows the identified database subject headings. When they find a good article, the librarian shows the student the associated subject terms so that the search can be modified to capture the most relevant sources of information.

Faculty are concerned about transfer students who are not doing as well as their peers who started at the institution as freshmen, particularly in writing research papers. A reference librarian develops an online interactive web tutorial that captures information about student performance, which can be shared with the instructors *and* with the feeder junior colleges. The subject librarians also target the 'gateway' course for each major specialty, and work with the associated instructors to develop a pathfinder for each course that will be linked to the online course management system. A multimedia presentation accompanies the pathfinder, and is also linked into the online course server.

Throughout the history of libraries, new technologies have drastically affected the way academic librarians perform reference and information services. As early as 1995, Richard Bazillion identified libraries as 'hi-tech' gateways (Bazillion and Braun, 2000). In the digital age, the nature of information has changed: in terms of access, format, interface, as well as the content itself. Therefore, intellectual access to this ever-increasing variety of information has also changed. Getting access, be it physical or digital is not enough: the academic community also has to understand the underlying principles of seeking knowledge. The way reference and instruction are conducted has shifted to meet the new needs of students and to address the new skills needed to navigate the rapidly expanding information highway. Lesley Moyo notes, 'during the last decade, many libraries, particularly those serving academic communities, have witnessed the emergence of new service paradigms in areas of information access and delivery, reference, instruction, technology facility and support to patrons' (Moyo, 2004: 220). As Web 1.0 turns into Web 2.0, the library has moved to the next level of service, meeting the growing reliance of society on technology. This chapter investigates how technological shifts have changed the way academic libraries address the needs of the academic community for intellectual access to their information needs.

The new college student

Much has been made of the coming of the Millennials, but how do they affect the way academic librarians approach intellectual access? Howe and Strauss (2003) describes the basic traits of students in this generation as sheltered, confident, team oriented, achieving, pressured and conventional. The Pew Report found that today's college students 'gather in groups and work in a computer lab ... Students were also observed positioning themselves at adjacent terminals in order to compare work on assignments easily' (Jones, 2002). In a protected environment, Millennials expect academic excellence and adhere to the norms presented to them. Perhaps the pressure to succeed felt by Millennials manifests itself in their attitudes towards academic honesty. Howe and Strauss (2000) found that students do not see cheating as a moral breach, which means the ease of copy and paste will only lend to that view and encourage such behaviour. Furthermore, this generation of students is even more focused on the instant gratification that technology affords them. Thomas Mann (1993) noted that students will often take the principle of least effort when searching for information; increased access only enables today's students to further rely on this principle when conducting research.

Research on Millennials provides insight for librarians regarding today's college students' use of technology and, more importantly, how they view the library. A 2002 Pew study found 'nearly three-quarters (73 per cent) of college students say they use the Internet more than the library, while only 9 per cent said they use the library more than the Internet for information searching'. Moreover, they found that 'students tend to use the Internet prior to going to the library to find information'. 'During direct observations of college students' use of the Internet in a library and in campus computer labs … the majority of students' time was not spent using the library resources online'. Given the lack of web design experience of many librarians it is not surprising that 'students in computer labs and classrooms were heard by observers to say that it is easier to find resources using the Internet' (Jones, 2002).

With the technological savvy found in this generation, there are still elements of undergraduate information seeking behaviour that remain constant despite their comfort level using e-mail, instant messaging, cell phones and social networking tools. Many studies have found students have problems mastering basic lower and higher-order research skills. Using observation and task analysis to determine where students have problems in the research process, researcher Mark Hepworth (1999) identified five main bottlenecks: defining the problem, defining where to go for information, developing search strategies, finding material in the library, developing insights, and extrapolation. He concluded that 'students found it difficult to place the problem (question) in the broader context; were unaware of the range of sources of information that could be used to identify relevant information; had a poor understanding of the 'information landscape; and creating search strategies proved difficult'.

Technology has amplified students' problems with the research process by giving them results on bad search terms, too many options for finding information, multiple search interfaces and of course too much information to process and synthesise.

From the reference desk to information commons

With the advent of digital technology, librarians have recognised the increased need for students to master certain foundational skills to function not only in an academic environment but also in the workplace. Discussions of information literacy have given way to information communication and technology (ICT) skills. The merging of critical thinking skills and technology skills is a new definition of information literacy in the academic library. To address this change, librarians have developed new paradigms of service in both reference and instruction.

While academic librarians have long believed the reference transaction is an ideal 'teachable moment', technology has underscored the need to revise the way librarians provide this service. Reference service design, transaction and pedagogy have been transformed over the last decade. Statistics have shown a lessening of traffic into the libraries, and reference desk statistics indicate a decline of in-person reference queries. For those who do use in-person reference services, the length of time spent on a single question has lengthened due to the complexities of access, explanation search strategies, and the number of sources available. Burke et al. (2005) found a direct correlation between increases in information literacy instruction with an increase in complexity of reference questions. As students become aware of various library resources, they recognise the need for more assistance with using them effectively.

In-person reference is being replaced increasingly by cyber access to librarians via 24/7 chat reference services, instant messaging, and e-mail reference. Remote use of library web pages (University of California, Los Angeles, Library, 2006), online research guides (Kent State University, 2006a), and digital library reference services demonstrate a growing importance of the digital library to students' lives. Likewise, academic libraries are utilising more innovative ways to reach students online. In the late 1990s, library gateway portals were considered cutting-edge; today they have been replaced by database-driven websites allowing customisable content and browser toolbars enabling instant access to library services without visiting the library homepage (University of Illinois Urbana-Champaign Library, 2006). E-tools such as blogs and podcasts are already giving way to MySpace library profiles and gaming technology for instruction. All of these emerging technologies indicate an effort to go 'virtually' to where the students are.

In the early 1990s, the California State University, Long Beach (CSULB) library held 6,000 print serial titles. Today, the library has 2,000 print titles and access to over 11,000 electronic titles. Similarly, large print collections such as the *Gale Literary Criticism* series and *Encyclopaedia Britannica* have been converted to searchable online formats that students can access remotely. In his article on the proliferation of electronic versions of classic references sources, Ken Winter (2000) identified at least six major publishers that converted titles to online sources. At CSULB, the number of titles physically in the reference collection has decreased by 60 per cent within the last five years.

The effect of technology extends beyond the format of reference titles, influencing the way librarians perform reference. Bradford et al. (2005) found that librarians at the University of Albany answered more than 60 per cent of their reference questions using electronic sources. Moreover, the percentage of reference questions answered by the print collection was just over 10 per cent. Even more surprising was that librarians used less than 2 per cent of the library's print reference collection to answer reference questions (Bradford et al., 2005).

With the growth of web-based resources, vendors have invested in more user-friendly interfaces and integrated tools targeted for the novice researcher, such as visual searching, citation generators, e-mail options and hyperlinked descriptors. Link resolvers such as Metalib and SFX make the entire search and retrieval process seamless to the end user. A by-product of this focus on end-user interface design is that librarians must orient the novice user to a variety of interfaces and steps not present in a traditional print source.

In an effort to accommodate access and the integration of library research with other academic skills, library reference areas are being transformed into information commons (IC). In her comprehensive evaluation of information commons facilities, Laurie MacWhinnie defines the IC as 'a central location within a library where access to technology and reference service is combined' (MacWhinnie, 2003: 241). Notable information commons include the Leavey Commons at University of Southern California, the Information Commons at the University of Arizona, and Uwill at the University of Washington. The next trend in the design of reference areas, from an information commons to learning commons, indicates reference is no longer the primary focus for service, but rather an integration of technology services is expected by students and the university.

A benefit of this trend is the opportunity for collaboration between the library and information technology units on campus. At CSULB, academic computing services were absorbed by the library, which includes control over the learning management system, Blackboard. This change permits the library to address one of the major issues involved in academic computing on all university campuses: interoperability. Likewise, the merger offers an opportunity for librarians to collaborate with teaching faculty to develop learning objects specifically designed to be integrated into the learning management system. Students will experience a seamless transition between learning platforms and access to library funded information sources.

The impact of technology on instruction

While just-in-time reference has usually included direct instruction, a more structured approach to library instruction has been a long-term effort by academic libraries. Not surprisingly, technology has also affected this library service. Traditionally, materials were hand-selected by librarians; now students have access to a multitude of un-evaluated materials. Since the evolution of information literacy as a concept, librarians have used instruction as a tool for teaching how to find, evaluate and apply information. As the complexity of research has grown, so has the recognition that information literacy should be a fundamental skill, much like quantitative reasoning and writing.

Similarly, academic libraries' technology-rich environment has increased the potential repertoire of instructional strategies, including interactive learning. Instructor computers and hands-on active learning have been joined by smartboards and personal response systems. Librarians have developed multiple methods for incorporating information competency skills at all levels.

General orientation

Even general orientations and the traditional library tours have also been affected by new technologies. There is an increased reliance on virtual tours; streaming video tours link from the library homepage to introduce students to basic layouts and locations of materials. The University of California at Los Angeles (UCLA) has been at the forefront for adopting new technologies for instruction and outreach; their podcasts and commercials (LiteBites) advertise the library, and provide instruction for basic search concepts. Library orientations now focus on services as well as locations as the combination of audio, video and HTML gives libraries the ability to provide additional context. The site Transition to College, a consortial effort developed at Kent State University, exemplifies the fusion of media for orientation purposes.

Standalone guides

With technology, academic librarians have been able to create general and specialised guides in a variety of formats: print, multimedia, video, web-based and wireless (for handheld devices). These guides offer instruction on scanning images, evaluating websites, searching databases, and so on. Online tutorials and other standalone web-based instruction products can provide interactive experiences related to information literacy processes. Since the creation of TILT in 1999, library tutorials have evolved alongside technology and new programming innovations. Flash and MySQL have facilitated the creation of visual and database-driven products that allow libraries unlimited access to students and faculty in distance learning environments, and the development of smaller modules of information to meet the just-in-time needs of the academic community. Flexibility and interactivity is evident in the latest generation of library tutorials; in 2002, North Carolina State University created a tutorial, LOBO, which allows students to login, record answers in a database, and send the answers to instructors.

Subsequently in 2004, CSULB modelled their tutorial, Students Understanding Research Fundamentals (SURF), on North Carolina's concepts. Targeting first-year students, the creators of SURF wanted to present library research in a fun and interesting format. Rather than merely presenting information, the tutorial allows students to identify their own research topic, and find resources that can be used on their own assignments. Students utilise a variety of interactive elements to visually clarify concepts and meet the needs of multiple learning styles. Both North Carolina and CSULB libraries established partnerships with faculty to ensure the effective use of their tutorials. They also used the tutorial databases to collect and analyse data for assessing student learning outcomes (California State University, Long Beach, Library, 2006).

Integrating information literacy instruction into courses

Course-integrated information literacy instruction has always been a major goal of academic library services. The advent of technology has meant a more concentrated effort to diversify the skills taught in an average session and the ability of the librarian to introduce a much more active learning environment. Personal response systems (PRS) and the use of wikis as learning tools are becoming more commonplace. PRS systems provide immediate feedback, and help gauge student knowledge during instruction, and wikis allow students to collaboratively build new knowledge (Matthies et al., 2006). Not only does an active learning environment cater to the technologically savvy Millennial students, it facilitates learning.

Many instructors ask students to find relevant articles, which has led academic librarians to demonstrate multiple database interfaces using a skills-based step-by-step approach to instruction. This approach led to the quandary of teaching this variety of skills in a 50-minute session. Librarians divided information into manageable chunks, a skill that is imperative for online tutorials and learning objects that may be considered as modular learning activities. Librarians have also transitioned from demonstrating technical skills to teaching concepts, thus eliminating the need to teach every nuance of every database. Focusing on the correct terminology and basic search structures also helps librarians get students started on the research process.

Information literacy in applied environments

One of the newer applications of information literacy has been to applied situations. New models of instruction including case-based problem-based learning, community of practice and peer-to-peer learning are all ways of increasing the use of skills and critical thinking in applied environments. With the rise of technology and the growth of information available in accessible electronic form, academic librarians recognise that information literacy skills are not limited to library resources. There has been a move to incorporate technology, media and visual literacy into the definition of information literacy.

Community service learning constitutes a significant venue for applying information competency. Such concrete learning venues increase student civic engagement, and also provide a motivation for applying information literacy skills in real-world situations. For example, the Information Competence Tutorial for the Discipline of Black Studies links each of the ACRL Information Literacy Standards to a service learning teaching unit (Luevano, Travis and Wakijii, 2004).

An extension of community service learning is actual workplace use of information communication and technology (ICT) skills. Christine Irving and John Crawford (2005) studied the acquisition of ICT skills and their subsequent usage in the workplace. In a survey of current and past graduates of Caledonian University in Glasgow, Scotland, they investigated the attitudes of students and alumni regarding the importance of information literacy in completing coursework or performing their job. Over 93 per cent of alumni considered that such skills were essential or of some use in their work. Their study indicates that information literacy is a useful lifelong learning skill.

A word about instructional design

As more courses are mounted electronically, the emphasis on instructional design has increased. Developed by industry human resource personnel with an eye on technology-enhanced training, instructional design is a structured way of looking at learner needs and creating learning activities that will help them meet desired outcomes. The most popular model, ADDIE, posits the following design steps:

- *Analysis*: What do students need, and what are their present skills?
- *Design*: What strategy will help students meet identified outcomes? How should content be organised? How should ideas be presented to learners? What delivery format should be used? What types of activities and exercises will best help learners? How should the course measure learners' accomplishments?
- *Development*: How should the strategy be 'packaged'? What resources are needed? Does content need to be created? How will the strategy be pilot-tested?
- *Implementation*: How will the activity be implemented? Where and when will it occur, and who is responsible for each aspect?
- *Evaluation*: What learning occurred? How effective was the instructional design planning and product? (Dick and Carey, 1996).

Academic librarians can use this model as a starting point in collaborating with teaching faculty, addressing information literacy needs in the process. For example, reference librarians constantly observe student information behaviour, and can provide valuable input about current competencies. Librarians can use their expertise about resources in developing relevant learning activities, and they can also share the reference interaction strategies that were effective in teaching students how to locate and evaluate information purposefully. Librarians should also strive to be included in evaluating student work in an effort to determine how to improve reference and information services.

Collaborating with teaching faculty to support intellectual access

The expertise of librarians in the area of using and teaching with technology provides a solid foundation for increasing their level of collaboration with faculty. Of course, differing degrees of collaboration exist in every university system depending upon status of the librarians and faculty culture. Many approaches have been taken by librarians to encourage and cultivate this phenomenon.

Setting the stage

Two pre-conditions must exist before information literacy based collaboration can exist: teaching faculty have to understand and value information literacy – and the academic librarian's role in curricular deployment. Technology adds another dimension in that it demands a change in the academic culture as well as in best practice. Counter-intuitively, change that involves technology requires significant psychological support and increased collaboration.

Most teachers prefer the status quo, and do not want to stray from their comfort zone. Thus, when confronted with information and technology literacy that is foreign to their experience – or if teachers have had a negative encounter with technology – they are not likely to change their behaviour.

Bloom's taxonomy of the affective domain posits five stages:

- *receiving*: getting and holding one's attention relative to information and technology literacy issues;

- *responding*: active participation and satisfaction in learning about information and technology;

- *valuing*: commitment to the underlying value of technology-infused information literacy;

- *organisation*: integration of possibly conflicting values to support information and technology literacy;

- *value complex*: pervasive and consistent incorporation of information and technology literacy (Krathwohl et al., 1973).

Typically, each stage needs to be addressed before the next stage can occur. At the initial stage of *awareness and receiving*, librarians have to gauge the present level of teachers' information literacy technology comfort and willingness to risk change and learn. Identifying areas in student achievement relative to intellectual access offers a solid foundation for discussion, and helps faculty advance to the next stage in Bloom's affective domain: *responding*.

Because teachers are then motivated to engage in activities that incorporate information literacy and technology to improve student learning, they are open to using electronic resources such as subscription databases and websites. They also see the use of workshops to learn how to incorporate information literacy explicitly. Of particular value are web-support systems and repositories such as Information Literacy for K-16 Settings (*http://www.csulb.edu/~lfarmer/infolitwebstyle.htm*) and Information Competence for the Discipline of Black Studies (*http://www.csulb.edu/~ttravis/BlackStudies/*).

By this point, faculty begin to *value* technology (Bloom's third stage within the affective domain), and seek ways to manage their learning and technology incorporation. Subject librarians should be poised to increase their presence during this process to facilitate joint course review and implementation of information literacy with technology enhancements. It should be noted that most teachers start with technology that helps their own teaching; afterwards, they feel more relaxed about using technology as a learning tool with their students. They also value developing a concrete *product* as a means to demonstrate authentic results. Throughout the process, academic librarians should probably emphasise close transfer of learning; thus, rather than providing generic information literacy direction, they should focus on domain-specific applications.

These efforts lead to the next stage in Bloom's taxonomy: *organisation*. This also signals readiness for deeper collaboration in support of programme-wide curriculum review and modification. Typical projects may include programmatic websites, information literacy rubrics, e-portfolio development and streaming video instruction, all of which foster consistent teaching and assessment across instructors. At this point, instructors can efficiently evaluate the quality of student work by means of online quizzes, and can regularly monitor student intellectual engagement in the subject matter through the use of online discussion groups.

The top stage in Bloom's taxonomy, *value complex*, is represented by an institutional commitment to intellectual access to information. At this stage, the entire academic community reflects a culture of intellectual access as evidenced by informational literacy graduation requirements, personnel decisions based on incorporation of information literacy into teaching, and a campus-wide infrastructure supporting these efforts.

In the final analysis, faculty development and technology incorporation are needed to provide a seamless articulation of information-rich learning so students will be successful *because students are the bottom line*. This mantra is a deeply-felt value that underlies the effort to change attitudes toward intellectual access to information. By taking advantage of such belief systems, academic librarians and teaching faculty can model and facilitate deep learning.

Degrees of collaboration

Providing resources in support of course curriculum is the most basic of services provided by librarians. Research guides, in-class assignments, and print handouts are established methods of assistance. Technology gives opportunity to expand the role of librarians as a partner in the educational process. Collaboration can range in breadth from one concept explained during a single class session to a programmatic approach to information literacy. Likewise, collaboration can range in depth from a single encounter to an ongoing professional relationship. Ideally, technology facilitates collaboration as telecommunications can facilitate asynchronous planning and documentation. However, when instructors are less comfortable with technology, the librarian may get the entire responsibility for teaching technical skills without any input from the instructor of record. Nevertheless, the extent of collaboration is usually less dependent on each party's technological expertise than it is on interpersonal trust.

Librarian as consultant

The consultant approach offers one way that academic librarians can assist faculty with infusing technology and information literacy skills into the curriculum. Consultation has been expanding from the role of a resource consultant to that of a joint creator of course content and delivery. Team-teaching models have been developed at the University of Hawaii, Guelph University in Canada, and Albany University (Hensley and Lebbin, 2002; Harrison et al., 2006; Bordonaro and Richardson, 2005). A uniquely advantageous aspect of this model is that librarians are also involved in the grading process unlike with a typical one-off session without seeing or assessing the students' final research. By making student learning outcomes a shared venture, instructors acknowledge the contributions of academic librarians to student success.

Learning management systems

Course management systems allow librarians the opportunity to develop learning objects for course-specific instruction. Beyond merely developing web pages or presentations to support an individual course, academic librarians can populate multiple sections with information literacy assignments or instruction. Librarians at San Diego State University are working with academic departments to create learning objects that can be incorporated into a course as it is created with the learning management system (Jackson, 2006).

University-wide initiatives

Increasingly, academic librarians are moving from an on-demand model of instruction to a concentrated effort to focus on curriculum development and university-wide requirements. The success of library instruction programmes is no longer measured by the number of course modules taught. More emphasis is being placed on reaching every student in a sequential and strategic manner. Rather than relying on the whim of an individual instructor to bring students to library sessions, librarians are working with curriculum committees and university administrators to insert information literacy and technology requirements into standard course outlines and general education policies. This approach removes the arbitrary nature of on-demand library instruction, and institutionalises the value of information literacy as a foundational skill rather than a library-specific initiative.

Assessing intellectual access

While academic librarians have incorporated technology into reference and instruction services, they have struggled with identifying how they are influencing student learning. As most academic librarians do not have the opportunity (or take it) to assess the student's work following a reference transaction or a one-off instruction session, technology-based assessments are being developed to address this problem. Libraries have long kept number tallies and conducted indirect assessments of library instruction; however, as they have become more involved in curriculum development and student learning outcomes, they have tried to find more formalised statistically valid measures of students' information literacy skills. On an institutional level, academic librarians strive to directly apply information literacy to student learning initiatives.

Standardised tests such as SAILS, PISA and the Educational Testing Services (ETS) ICT test have been created to asses the technical and information literacy skills of students and, as a corollary, the university's effectiveness in teaching those skills. These tests have different foci and applicability to the university setting. Based upon the Association of College and Research Library information literacy standards, SAILS is a multiple-choice test that measures undergraduate students' acquisition of information literacy skills (Kent State University, 2006b). By contrast, the ICT test developed by the Educational Testing Services (2006) and the international PISA assessment are broader in scope, measuring not only information literacy skills but also computer literacy and critical thinking skills. The ETS test takes 75 minutes to complete, and is available only in a controlled proctored environment. All of these tests address the information competencies of defining, accessing, evaluating, integrating, creating and communicating. These standardised tests also demonstrate the growing importance of assessing intellectual access in an academic environment.

Challenges to consider

With the benefits of technology in fostering intellectual access, there are issues that librarians need to consider, such as the changing nature of library work, the cost of electronic collections and the cost of maintaining technology tools.

Librarianship has become a profession that is defined by technological change: from card catalogues to DOS-based Dialog searches, to the Internet. New librarians are expected to possess knowledge of emerging technologies in addition to traditional library skills. Experience with instructional design, programming and remote services to users is increasingly listed on job descriptions. Technological innovation has 'created an ascendant class of librarians and non-librarians with technological mastery, while librarians with traditional skills have suffered a relative loss in status' (Bazillion and Braun, 2000: 24). Thus, training for new products and staying abreast of new technologies via professional development takes a large portion of a librarian's time. To avoid becoming dinosaurs, academic librarians must remain competitive by being open to technological change.

Training has become another important component of technology. The increasing information commons has meant a diversification in skills needed by all levels of staff. Allison Cowgill documents the training and planning involved at Colorado State University when they moved from a library environment to an information commons model. She found that 'It is crucial that staff feel comfortable with their new responsibilities and are able to provide solid assistance in this very technological and rapidly changing environment' (Cowgill et al., 2001: 438).

Newer reference services also take a larger portion of time. E-mail reference and virtual chat are more time-consuming that traditional reference. A study of chat reference queries found that on average most transactions lasted 144 minutes, and some lasted as long as 33 minutes (Walter and Mediavilla, 2005). Lee (2004) found that chat transactions took 600 per cent longer than an in-person reference transaction, with an online transaction taking 163 words and seven minutes while the in-person transaction would have taken approximately 70 seconds.

The shift to electronic resources in the reference collection allows 24/7 access to students and faculty but it can be very expensive. Print titles are a one-time permanent purchase while leased content of electronic databases and reference collections means that any funding deficits might mean the loss of access. Continually, libraries choose convenience for users over the security of ownership.

Indeed, keeping the library connected consumes a large portion of library funding. Maintenance includes computer hardware, updating applications and ensuring the appropriate security is installed. As stated previously, interoperability of applications, software and hardware requires constant testing and technical expertise. Nevertheless, true cost-benefit analyses of these emerging technologies are hard to find, particularly with regard to intellectual access. Monitoring usage of services and e-tools should be built into technology planning.

Conclusion

Technology, information literacy and access to information continue to be at the forefront of planning for academic library reference and information services. In today's academic setting, such planning has moved outside of the library to become recognised as a foundational need for students throughout their academic and social lives. If the library wants to remain an influential part of this trend, there needs to be a transition from the library as *place* to the library as *teaching unit*, an entity that facilitates student learning, enabling foundation critical thinking and the creation of new knowledge.

7

Technology impact on evaluating reference and information services

Lesley Farmer

The merits of evaluating reference and information services are obvious. If the library does not effectively carry out its mission in support of the institution, the institution is less likely to support the library. In an academic environment, reference librarians can act as reflective action researchers as they assess their services. In the digital age, technology becomes both a subject of evaluation as well as a means to evaluate reference services. One key to its successful incorporation is the human element: the values, knowledge and skill set of the entire library staff.

A systems approach to evaluation

Reference librarians continuously evaluate resources and services. In every reference transaction, the reference librarian assesses the user and their information needs, available resources, personal ways to interact with the user. If possible, the reference librarian also follows up the interaction to find out if the user was able to answer their information question. Likewise, as reference librarians instruct, they observe student behaviour and adjust their content delivery to ensure that students can understand and apply the information skills. Even a saunter through the reference book or a quick perusal of an online reference bibliography gives rise to the identification of reference gaps that need to be addressed.

Library reference and information services can be evaluated in a straightforward manner. It is easy to track people using library services, even online. Academic community 'products' – student work, faculty publications, service to the community – are routinely reviewed publicly. Nevertheless, ferreting out the direct impact that library reference and information services make on the academic community over time can be challenging. A more feasible approach to assess the library's overall impact is to examine each element that supports the institution's mission.

In short, a systematic approach to evaluating reference and information services is key to optimising improvement. The entire library staff – and relevant stakeholders – need to be involved in developing and implementing an evaluation plan. As important, evaluation needs to be an ongoing activity that informs all reference services. Other principles of good assessment include using a variety of methods to capture different perspectives at different points in time, considering both process and products, assessing on an ongoing basis, and considering assessment as integral to the big picture (Astin et al., 1992).

Whitlatch (2000), on behalf of the American Library Association's Reference and User Services Association (RUSA), enumerated best practices in evaluating reference and information services:

- Determine the extent that reference services align with and support institutional goals and academic community information needs.

- Determine how well institutional resources are allocated and used to support the implementation of library reference services.

- Evaluate services in light of users' perceived priorities: timeliness, behaviour, accessibility, value, effectiveness.

- Evaluate reference sources as a unified collection, including all formats in-house and those that are accessible by library users.

- Use a variety of evaluation methods, both formal and informal. Compare data with comparable institutions and established standards.

Evaluation should occur at every level. Obviously, the library staff first need to know the institution's mission and goals. However, subject librarians should find out about each college, department and programme's mission, goals and standards. Service unit charges, such as health and career development, should also be identified. At each operational level, reference librarians should assess the relevant input personnel, material resources and services/actions available to work with.

- *personnel*: the academic community's prior subject and reference/information-related skills, knowledge, and dispositions;

- *curriculum*: desired outcomes, standards, content matter frameworks, 'canon' documents, trends;

- *resources*: documents, money, technology, facilities supporting academics;

- *instruction*: methods, delivery channels, timeframe, learning activities, grading practices;

- *collaboration*: degree, extent, and nature of collaboration between teaching faculty, and between teaching faculty and reference librarians;

- *governance*: how academic decisions are made and resources allocated.

Reference librarians need to ascertain which resources may affect library reference and information services, or are affected by the library.

Likewise, output indicators also need to be examined in order to determine how the library's reference and information services affect the academic community:

- *students*: application of information literacy, greater content knowledge, improved academic standing, higher retention and graduation rates, future employment;

- *teaching faculty*: greater productivity, higher student evaluations, more effective collaboration, increased research and scholarly activity quality and quantity, more effective service, increasing number and remuneration of grants and awards, higher retention and tenure rates;

- *service personnel*: greater productivity, more support, more resource allocations, improved institutional governance, increasing number and remuneration of grants and awards, more effective collaboration, more effective partnerships with the community;

- *administration*: greater productivity, more effective collaboration, improved institutional governance, increasing number and remuneration of grants and awards, improved fiscal picture, more effective partnerships with the community, higher comparative institutional rankings.

By ascertaining potential input and output factors, reference librarians can determine which venues to pursue. Which reference and information services does the library uniquely provide? What expertise do reference librarians possess that contributes uniquely to the institution's wellbeing? While this initial assessment can be done entirely by the library staff, it is important to involve the major stakeholders in this investigation, as their perceptions will affect the effectiveness of the library's reference and information services. For instance, if the reference librarians spend substantial resources on helping students find jobs, and a career centre thinks it is doing a fine job of this, then the library is probably stepping on toes; if they really want to help in that arena, they would be more effective if they collaborated with the existing support service. Likewise, if reference librarians spend more of their instructional time teaching students how to do annotated bibliographies, but the teaching faculty do not ask students to do such work, all parties will be frustrated.

Starting with the community

Fundamentally, the reference/information service evaluation plan should begin with the academic community and the institution's goals, and the reference functions that support that community. What does each entity bring – and want – from the reference 'table'? The library's vision should align with the institution's mission, with the idea that reference services and resources carry out part of the library's vision. In that spirit, library staff need to assess their constituents – the academic community and sometimes the community at large – in light of the library's contribution to their informational welfare.

- What are the desired outcomes?
- What are the standards of performance?
- What are the indicators that demonstrate meeting the outcomes?
- How are the indicators measured?
- What resources and actions/services facilitate meeting the outcomes?

Librarians can gather data about the community in several ways:

- *publications*: institutional policies, programmes of study, annual reports, committee charges and meeting minutes, websites, faculty resumés, sample student work;

- *datasets*: student management systems, library management systems, faculty data, alumni data;
- *observations*: academic community behaviours throughout the campus and online;
- *surveys and questionnaires*: student evaluations of faculty, community satisfaction surveys, alumni and employer surveys, programmatic and departmental surveys;
- *interviews*: of stakeholders individually and in focus groups.

It should be noted, that data collected by the library might well fit into this data collection: library visit counts, reference fill-rate surveys, circulation records, library web portal and database 'hits,' digital reference transaction archives, and any other data that indicate community interaction with the reference programme.

While the explicit intent of data sources might be totally separate from the library, the *analysis* of the data uses a reference service perspective. Some of the guiding questions follow:

- What are the information needs of the academic community?
- How are those information needs met, both in terms of resources and services?
- What information competencies does the academic community need?
- What information competencies do they demonstrate?
- What resources and actions/services help the academic community become information literate?
- What role does the library play in meeting information needs of the academic community?

By identifying the informational needs and the capabilities of the academic community, as well as the available institutional resources and services to support informational goals, the library staff can align its efforts more effectively.

Technology-enhanced reference and information service standards

In 2000, RUSA developed a set of guidelines to assess reference and information services (Whitlatch, 2000). The key components can be aligned to assess the library services' impact on the academic community's information goals. When electronic technology is incorporated into reference and information services, the standards 'bar' is raised:

- *Services*: Meet and anticipate user information needs. Answer queries completely and accurately. Provide instruction and information aids (e.g. signs, maps, flyers, tutorials). Develop and disseminate library service policies. Promote information services. With technology, services should be more responsive to user needs in terms of customised and timely service. Instruction should employ a variety of formats and delivery modes. Dissemination and promotion of services should reach the entire academic community equitably.

- *Resources*: Locate and collect reference resources that meet and anticipate user information needs. Package and create information to meet users' informational needs. Develop and implement reference access and collection policies. With technology, needs should be identified more effectively. Information packaging and creation should incorporate more formats, and be more customised, to address individual needs and learning preferences. Policies should be developed collaboratively, and incorporate technology aspects.

- *Access*: Plan and implement an efficient organisation of reference resources and services. Support current communication methods, including relevant technology. Provide physical and virtual access operating hours aligned with user information needs. Ensure access to outside information through participation in consortia and networks. With technology, planning should include technology both as a means and as an end.

- *Personnel*: Provide a sufficient number of qualified staff to meet user information needs. Communicate effectively with all users. Hire, train and develop library staff who are knowledgeable about information, information processes, and interpersonal skills. Model ethical behaviour. With technology, personnel should be technologically competent, and staff development should incorporate technology methods and content.

In order to implement high-quality reference services, the library's leadership and infrastructure need to be effective. Breivik and Gee (2006) identified the following information management components that need to be evaluated. Again, technology impacts management standards:

- *Control of budget allocations*: Technological tools should improve planning and oversight of finances.

- *Acquisitions policies and procedures*: Automated library management systems should inform acquisitions decisions and facilitate information lifecycle management

- *Management of reference services*: Automated library management systems and personnel management software should optimise deployment of library staff.

- *Involvement of community*: Telecommunications should facilitate community communication, planning, implementation and dissemination of results.

- *Policies and their accountability/enforcement*: Technology should foster broad-based policy development and improve oversight of policy compliance.

- *Collaboration with other libraries/agencies*: Technology standardisation (e.g. Z39.50) and telecommunications should facilitate joint initiatives.

- *Accreditation*: Technology should facilitate programme development and assessment efforts (Breivik and Gee, 2006, 220).

Several indicators show that technology is effectively used in academic reference and information services to support the institution's mission:

- the library uses technology effectively to develop and maintain the collection and access to other information resources;

- institutional facilities, including the library, support access and use of digital information;

- the academic community, including library staff, uses digital information effectively and purposefully in communication, teaching and learning, and service;

- information behaviour improves as a result of incorporating technology;

- the institution plans and provides material and human support for technology-enhanced reference and information services;

- the academic community, including library staff, partners effectively with community entities to advance joint initiatives.

Likewise, ineffective technology usage can be perceived through:

- lack of technology use to meet information needs;
- inappropriate use of technology to meeting information needs (e.g. cut-and-paste plagiarism);
- greater focus on technology features than on content enhancement;
- outdated or unstable technology;
- limited digital resources;
- lack of institutional planning and support for technology-enhanced reference and information services (Loertscher, 2000: 152–3).

Evaluation tools

To measure how well academic library reference and information services meet professional standards, valid and reliable assessment instruments must be administered. The basic questions about assessment practices endure:

- Who will assess? Who is being assessed?
- How will assessment be done?
- Where will assessment be done: in the library, in classrooms, on campus, virtually?
- When will assessment be done: at what stage; what timeframe?
- Why is assessment being done: to describe, to improve, to show impact?

However, technology has expanded the possibilities of evaluation because it can 'collapse' time and space, greatly expand access, combine media, increase interactivity and facilitate repurposing of data. Examples of technology tools that can be used for assessment include:

- survey templates and repurposing;
- sortable databases;
- spreadsheets for analysis;
- handheld devices for quick observation and feedback;
- telecommunications for collaborative work such as joint view of documents in an asynchronous, cross-platform, secure environment;
- video/images for capturing scenarios.

With the advent of electronic technology, academic librarians have changed assessment approaches. Some of their current practices follow:

- preference for performance assessment;
- transition from tool-based to problem-based assessment;
- transition from library-centric to content-centric assessment;
- transition from multiple choice standardised tests to portfolios of evidence;
- tension between high stakes testing and ongoing assessment;
- acknowledgment of the affective domain's role in information literacy assessment;
- collaborative assessment between academic and teaching faculty;
- use of simulations;
- incorporation of technology;
- embedded assessment within tutorials to give instant feedback and targeted remediation;
- investigation of system-wide conditions for information literacy learning (Farmer and Henri, 2007).

United National Educational, Scientific and Cultural Organization Bangkok (2006) developed a very thorough set of information and communication technology indicators, sample assessment tools and related questionnaires categorised by governance level:

- policy and strategy;
- infrastructure and access;
- curriculum and textbooks;
- teaching professionals' use and teaching;
- students' use and learning.

These tools can be easily adapted by reference librarians to examine their impact.

Action research

The act of evaluation in itself is not very productive; its value lies in acting upon the data generated. Action research is one viable way to improve library reference service. This practical research methodology focuses on improving the current reference service situation. This process may also be considered a cycle of enquiry as the results lead to continuous improvement. When reference librarians identify an arena for focus, they:

- research the underlying issues and possible solutions that other people have tried;
- develop research questions to answer;
- gather data to get baseline information;
- recommend interventions based on the literature review and the situational data;
- implement interventions;
- assess interventions to determine their effectiveness.

This kind of research supports the idea of reflective practice, and also serves as a way for reference librarians to engage in meaningful research in an academic setting. Ideally, librarian researchers will collaborate with the teaching faculty peers in conducting reference-related research as a way to integrate information behaviours into academic conversation. By aligning domain-specific and information literacy outcomes with instructional strategies and methods of assessment, both parties can improve their contributions to student learning.

Technology can enhance action research efforts at each stage. Certainly, academic librarians can search the literature and access a broader spectrum of relevant assessment tools more efficiently with technology. Data gathering and analysis benefit from electronic tools that can be easily exported for statistical analysis. Telecommunications facilitates the development and deployment of feasible interventions. Particularly as digital data can be transformed and repurposed relatively easily, stakeholders can all work as a team to optimise reference and information services in support of the institution's mission.

A case study in information literacy assessment

Kelly Janousek's collaboration with the Public Policy and Administration (PPA) Department in support of information literacy exemplifies an interactive evaluation process that improved technology-related reference and information services. At California State University Long Beach (CSULB), Janousek serves as subject reference librarian for PPA. Noticing the growth in the department's course offerings and the decline in information literacy instruction, she collaborated with PPA faculty to apply for a system information competency grant to identify basic information outcomes required for all graduate students, to incorporate information literacy instruction and learning activities strategically into courses throughout the programme, and to assess students' success in demonstrating those outcomes.

To support that effort, a workshop was developed for PPA teaching faculty to understand the role of information competency in their programme. On the library's part, reference materials were purchased, and the corresponding subject library website research guide was also expanded and updated. A three-hour library information class PowerPoint presentation was developed and implemented to cover research strategies, reference resources, source citation and research help. The student product indicator was an annotated bibliography.

In analysing the resultant bibliographies, Janousek discovered several areas for improvement: library catalogue access to government information, the citation finding program SFX retrieval of PPA-related journal articles, the library collection to support PPA. In terms of instruction, students needed more guidance in identifying significant citation details and in evaluating potential resources. The information session and related website also needed to show the research pathway more clearly. As a result of the assessment, instruction was adjusted to provide a more integrated approach to reference sources and more explicit instruction on formatting research reports. Janousek has noticed that department 'students are now asking more savvy questions, and the need for individual research consultation has declined' (Janousek, 2006).

Appendix: New database form

Web team checklist

___Instructional guide template, if requested by sponsor, available at *http://www.csulb.edu/library/instruction/handouts/*

___Info box added to */library/test/Boxes/*, */library/eref/Boxes/*, and *refnet.library.csulb.edu/Boxes/*

___Target for RefWorks instructions will be _____

___Added to */library/test/testproducts.html*

___Added to EzProxy config file and/or _____password page added to password server

___Verified that database works remotely

___Database added to */eref.html* and */topic.html*

___Target on alpha *eref.html* is *http://www.csulb.edu/library/eref/eref .html#*

___Librarians, info programs, and webgroup notified of availability

___Campus community update prepared

___Product added to 'what's new', website indexes

___Completed form distributed to:

    ___Serials Accountant (database information.xls [including topics and tech info tabs] and admin accounts.xls)

    ___Electronic Resource Manager (Serials Solutions, SFX, Metalib and library catalogue information)

    ___Acquisitions Coordinator

___If product replaces something, pre-existing product has been edited off of appropriate listings

___Completion date _____

Product sponsor

Date: _____

Sponsor's name: _____

Title: _____

Content: Full text ____PDF/Adobe ____Citation/Abstract ____
Some full text____

Database information (for 'about' boxes):

- Description (content):
- Coverage (years):
- How frequently updated:
- Number of simultaneous users:

Database is a consortium-licensed product:
Yes ____ No ____

Database is a consortium Electronic Core Collection product:
Yes ____ No ____

Recommendation for website listings (please indicate as appropriate):
_____ Only to be represented by Serials Solutions MARC records (automatically done for ALL full text databases) and via SFX (if available as an SFX target).

For Topics Pages: Place a check to the right of each topic page for which you recommend listing this database. The subject specialists will be contacted by the database coordinator to determine: (1) their interest in listing, and (2) the topics page listing sequence:

If you wish to list the database ONLY on the A-Z list, please check here:

_____

Topic page	Recommended	Accepted
Anthropology		
Art/Art History/Design		
Biography		
Biology		
Business		
Chemistry/Biochemistry		
Child & Family Studies		
Communication Studies		
Companies		
Computer Science		
Consumer Affairs		
Criminal Justice		
Dance		
Dissertations/Theses		
Economics		
Education		
Electronic Books		
Encyclopedias/Dictionaries		
Engineering		
Environment/Ecology		
Ethnic Studies		
Fashion Design/Merchand.		
FCS Education		
Film/Television		
Food Science		
General/Interdisciplinary		
Geography/Maps		
Geology		
GerontologyHealth/Medical/Nursing		
History		
Hotel Mgmt./Hospitality		
Human Development		
Humanities		
Industries		
International Business		
International Relations		
Journalism		
Kinesiology/Physical Edu		
Language/Linguistics		

continued

Topic page	Recommended	Accepted
Law/Legislation		
Library & Info Science		
Literature		
Mathematics & Statistics		
Music		
Newspapers		
Nutrition/Dietetics		
Philosophy		
Physics		
Political Science		
Psychology		
Public Policy & Admin		
Public Relations		
Recreation & Leisure		
Religion		
Social Sciences		
Social Work		
Sociology		
Statistics		
Theatre Arts		
Women & Gender Studies		

Product URL:

_____

Launch URL:

_____

(Only necessary to include if you prefer to launch the database from other than its start page. You will need to verify with the vendor that you can use this URL.)

Database Instruction Guide: (if you are NOT developing a local instruction guide via Omni template, please provide here the URL for the vendor's help/instruction page.) Note: this needs to be a static or persistent URL. If you see 'session' somewhere in the url string, it will not be persistent! _____

Authentication method:

___by IP Address ___by Password ____ by both IP and Password

> When speaking with your vendor re: IP restrictions, please provide them with the following IP domain: 100.100.*.* This will restrict access to any computer on campus or via the proxy.

User IDs or passwords (if used): _____

Does this product replace a web product to which we already subscribe? Yes ____ No ____

- Name of product to be replaced: _____
- When can old product be removed? _____

Technical information (information for sponsor to get from vendor)

Note: if this vendor is one of our 'standard' vendors (e.g. FirstSearch, EBSCO, etc.), it is not necessary to complete this section (just enter vendor name as the contact information will be the same). If you are not sure if this applies to your database, contact Sara.

Vendor information (If all of the following vendor information is provided on a single web page, please just list the web page.)

The information we would like to have is: Name (customer service rep or your contact – not all orgs will have this); Phone; E-mail; Technical Support Phone; Technical Support E-mail; Technical Support Webpage:

Database can be implemented in SFX (vendor's language for this may vary: supports the open URL standard, offers a link resolver, uses DOI, etc.):

- SOURCE (indexing database): Yes ____ No ____ Not Sure ____
- TARGET (full text database): Yes ____ No ____ Not Sure ____

(You can check re: Sources at *http://www.exlibrisgroup.com/sfx_sources.htm* and for Targets at *http://www.exlibrisgroup.com/sfx_targets.htm* – If after looking at these links, you are not sure, just check 'Not Sure' Sara will verify and let you know)

Database offers an export function that allows direct export to RefWorks or provides a mechanism for exporting to bibliographic management software such as EndNote. Yes _____ No _____

Database has an administrative module that can be manipulated locally to make changes in the interface, searching, logoff location, etc. or can be used to gather usage statistics. (Note: many of our existing vendors – FirstSearch, EBSCO, etc. – have this.) Yes _____ No _____

If the answer is YES, please provide logon procedures (URL, username/password, etc): _____

Note: If the following four questions are not addressed on the vendor's technical support web page, then copy and paste these questions into an e-mail and send to technical support.

1. Which browser versions are supported? (please indicate version numbers)

- Internet Explorer: _____
- Netscape: _____
- Firefox: _____
- Safari: _____
- Opera: _____
- Is there a preferred browser: _____

(some vendors will say both work, but one works 'better')

2. Is the database compliant with Section 508 and/or the Americans with Disabilities Act? Yes _____ No _____

(Note: if the database is produced outside of the USA contact the database coordinator for alternative applicable language.)

3. Can vendor supply a link to a statement regarding the above? If vendor says the database is not compliant or does not have a link to a

statement please ask when they anticipate compliance or when they anticipate having a web-based statement?

4. Is there any additional software that must be installed in order for this database to work successfully? Yes _____ No _____

If yes, please explain:_____

Sponsor: Please add below any other information that you believe will be helpful (e.g. copy/paste of e-mail correspondence with the vendor and/or their tech support people). THANK YOU!

Bibliography

Allard, S., Mack, T. and Feitner-Reichert, M. (2005) 'The librarian's role in institutional repositories: A content analysis of the literature', *Reference Services Review*, 33(3): 325–36.

American Medical Association (2004) *Family Medical Guide* (4th edn), New York: John Wiley and Sons.

Astin, A., Banta, T., Cross, K., El-Khawas, E., Ewell, P., Hutchings, P., Marchese, T., McClenney, K., Mentkowski, M., Miller, M., Moran, E. and Wright, B. (1992) *Nine Principles of Good Practice for Assessing Student Learning*, Washington, DC: American Association of Higher Education.

Astin, A., Oseguera, L., Sex, L. and Korn, W. (2002) *The American Freshmen: Thirty-five Year Trends, 1966–2001*, Los Angeles: Higher Education Research Institute, UCLA.

Atton, C. (1994) 'Using critical thinking as a basis for library user education', *The Journal of Academic Librarianship*, 20(5/6): 310–13.

Bazillion, R. and Braun, C. (2000) *Indigenous Archaeology: American Indian Values and Scientific Practice*, Chicago: American Library Association.

Bejune, M. and Kinkus, J. (2006) 'Creating a composite of user behavior to inform decisions about new and existing library services', *Reference Services Review*, 34(2): 185–92.

Bordonaro, K. and Richardson, G. (2004) 'Scaffolding and reflection in course-integrated library instruction', *The Journal of Academic Librarianship*, 30: 391–401.

Borek, D., Bell, B., Richardson, G. and Lewis, W. (2006) 'Perspectives on building consortia between libraries and other agencies', *Library Trends*, 54(3): 448–62.

Borgman, C. (1996) 'Why are online catalogs still hard to use?' *Journal of the American Society for Information Science and Technology*,

47(7): 493–503.

Boss, R. W. (2005) 'Library portals', *Tech Notes*, available at *http://www.ala.org/ala/pla/plapubs/technotes/librarywebportals.htm* (accessed 28 September 2006).

Bradford, J., Barbara C. and Lenholt, R. (2005) 'Reference service in the digital age: An analysis of sources used to answer reference questions', *The Journal of Academic Librarianship*, 31: 263–72.

Breivik, P. and Gee, G. (2006) *Higher Education in the Internet Age*, Westport, CT: Praeger.

Budapest Open Access Initiative (2002) available at *http://www.soros.org/openaccess/read.shtml* (accessed 28 September 2006).

Burke, G., Germain, C. and Xu, L. (2005) 'Information literacy: Bringing a renaissance to reference', *Portal: Libraries and the Academy*, 5: 353–70.

Byrne, A. (2005) 'Promoting the global information commons', available at *http://www.ifla.org/III/wsis/wsis-24Feb05.html* (accessed 28 September 2006).

California Library Association (2005) 'Technology core competencies for California library workers', available at *http://www.cla-net.org/included/docs/tech_core_competencies.pdf* (accessed 28 September 2006).

California State University, Long Beach, Library (2006) 'SURF: Students Understanding Research Fundamentals', available at *http://nike.cecs.csulb.edu/~surf* (accessed 28 September 2006).

Carlson, S. (2005) 'The net generation goes to college', *The Chronicle of Higher Education*, 52(7): A34–A37.

Carlson, S. (2006) 'Library renovation leads to soul searching at Cal Poly', *Chronicle of Higher Education*, 53(2): A59.

Case, O. (2002) *Looking for Information: A survey of Research on Information Seeking, Needs and Behaviors*, New York: Academic Press.

Chan, D., Kwok, C. and Yip, S. (2005) 'Changing roles of reference librarians: the case of the HKUST Institutional Repository', *Reference Services Review*, 33(3): 268–82.

Cortwright, R., Collins, H. and DiCarlo, S. (2005) 'Peer instruction enhanced meaningful learning: Ability to solve novel problems', *Advances in Physiology Education*, 29(2): 107–11.

Cowgill, A., Beam, J. and Wess, L. (2001) 'Implementing an information commons in a university library', *Journal of Academic Librarianship*, 27: 432–39.

Crawford, J. (2006) 'The use of electronic information services and information literacy: A Glasgow Caledonian University study', *Journal of Librarianship and Information Science,* 38: 33–8.

Crawford, W. (2002) 'The Crawford files', *American Libraries,* 33(4): 91.

Dick, W. and Carey, L. (1996) *The Systematic Design of Instruction* (4th edn), New York: Harper Collins.

DiMattia, S. (2005) 'Silence is olden', *American Libraries,* 36(1): 48–51.

Driscoll, L. (2003) *Electronic Reserve: A Manual and Guide for Library Staff Members,* New York: Haworth Press.

Duck, P. and Koeske, R. (2005) 'Marketing the millennials: What they expect from their library experience', paper presented at the ACRL 12th National Conference: Currents and Convergence: Navigating the Rivers of Change, Minneapolis, MN, October.

Educational Testing Service (2006) 'ICT literacy assessment information and communication technology literacy', available at *http://www.ets.org* (accessed 28 September 2006).

Farb, S. and Riggio, A. (2004) 'Medium or message? A new look at standards, structures and schemata for managing electronic resources', *Library Hi Tech,* 22(2): 144–52.

Farmer, L. (2005) *Technology-Infused Instruction for the Educational Community,* Lanham, MD: Scarecrow Press.

Farmer, L. and Henri, J. (2007) *Information Literacy and Assessment,* Lanham, MD: Scarecrow Press.

Fernandez, L. (2002) 'User perceptions of current awareness services: A faculty survey', *Issues in Science and Technology Librarianship,* (Winter), available at *http://www.istl.org/02-winter/article3.html* (accessed 28 September 2006).

Harrison, J. Rourke, L. and Burpee, K. (2006) 'The benefits of buy-in: Integrating information literacy into each year of an academic program', paper presented at LOEX of the West 2006, Kona, Hawaii, June.

Hensley, R. and Lebbin, V. (2002) 'Learning communities for first-year undergraduates: connecting the library through credit courses', in J. Nims and A. Andrew (eds), *First Impressions, Lasting Impact: Introducing the First-year Student to the Academic Library,* Ann Arbor, MI: Pierian Press.

Hepworth , M. (1999) 'A study of undergraduate information literacy and skills: the inclusion of information literacy and skills in the undergraduate curriculum', paper presented at IFLA conference, Bangkok, August.

Hicks, R. and Hicks, K. (1999) *Boomers, Xers and Other Strangers:*

Understanding the Generational Differences that Divide Us, Wheaton, IL: Tyndale House.

Holliday, W. and Li, Q. (2004) 'Understanding the millennials: Updating our knowledge about students', *Reference Services Review*, 32(4): 356–66.

Howe, N. and Strauss, W. (2000) *Millennials Rising*. New York: Vintage Books.

Howe, N. and Strauss, W. (2003) *Millennials Go to College*. Washington DC: The American Association of Collegiate Registrars and Admissions Officers.

International Federation of Library Associations, Reference and Information Service Section (2006) 'Strategic plan 2006–2007', available at *http://www.ifla.org/VII/s36/annual/sp36.htm* (accessed 28 September 2006).

Irving, C. and Crawford, J. (2005) 'From secondary school to the world of work: the experience of evaluating information literacy skills development at Glasgow Caledonian University (GCU)', *JeLit*, 2(2), available at *http://www.jelit.org/66/* (accessed 10 November 2006).

Jackson, P. (2006) 'Information literacy student learning packets', available at *http://infodome.sdsu.edu/infolit/learningpackets.shtml* (accessed 29 September 2006)

Janousek, K. (2006) 'Around it goes: From grant development to program assessment for an information competence program in public policy and administration graduate program', paper presented at the Southern California Instruction Librarians Program, San Marcos, CA, February.

Jassin, M. (2005) 'The flat track to new career options for information professionals', *Online*, 29(5): 22–4.

Jones, S. (2002) 'The Internet goes to college; How students are living in the future with today's technology', available at *http://www .pewinternet.org/PPF/r/71/report_display.asp* (accessed 25 September 2006).

Katz, W. (2001) *Introduction to Reference Work* (8th edn), New York: McGraw-Hill.

Kent State University (2006a) 'Transitioning to college: Helping you succeed', available at from *http://www.transitioning2college.org/* (accessed 9 September 2006).

Kent State University (2006b) 'Project SAILS', available at *https://www .projectsails.org/sails/aboutSAILS.php?page=aboutSAILS* (accessed 9 September 2006).

Kinnersley, R. T. (2000) 'Electronic resources in Kentucky secondary schools: A survey of availability and instruction for students', *Internet Reference Services Quarterly*, 5(1): 7–28.

Kleiner, J. P. (1993) 'The electronic library: The hub of the future's information networks', *The Reference Librarian*, 39: 131–9.

Krathwohl, D., Bloom, B. and Bertram, B. (1973) *Taxonomy of Educational Objectives, The Classification of Educational Goals. Handbook II: Affective Domain*, New York: David McKay.

Lawrence, S. (2001) 'Online or invisible?' *Nature*, 411(6837): 521.

Lee, I. (2004) 'Do virtual reference librarians dream of digital reference questions? A qualitative and quantitative analysis of email and chat reference', *Australian Academic and Research Libraries*, 35: 95–110.

Lenhart, A. (2001) *Teenage Life Online*, Washington, DC: Pew Internet & American Life Project.

Leo, J. (2003) 'The good-news generation', *US News and World Report*, 135(15): 60.

Library Technology Reports (2005) 'Integration of libraries and course-management systems' *Library Technology Reports*, 41(3): 12–20.

Lodge, M. (2004) 'Services to persons with disabilities: Libraries respond', *Ohio Libraries*, 17(2): 26–7.

Loertscher, D. (2000) *Taxonomies of the School Library Media Program* (2nd edn), San Jose, CA: Hi Willow.

Luevano, S., Travis, T. and Wakijii, E. (2004) 'Information competence for the discipline of Black studies', available at *http://www.csulb .edu/~ttravis/BlackStudies/* (accessed 28 September 2006).

Lupien, P. (2006) 'Virtual reference in the age of pop-up blockers, firewalls and service pack 2', *Online*, 30(4): 14–19.

MacWhinnie, L. (2003) 'The information commons: The academic library of the future', *Portal: Libraries and the Academy*, 3: 241.

Mann, T. (1993) *Library Research Models: A Guide to Classification, Cataloging and Computers*, New York: Oxford University Press.

Markus, L. (2001) 'Toward a theory of knowledge reuse: Types of knowledge reuse situations and factors in reuse success', *Journal of Management Information Systems*, 18(1): 57–93.

Martin, K. (2006) 'Moving into the digital age: A conceptual model for a publications repository', *Internet Reference Services Quarterly*, 11(2): 27–47.

Matthies, B., Helmke, J. and Slater, P (2006) 'Using a wiki to enhance library instruction', *Indiana Libraries*, 25(3): 32–4.

McLean, N. and Lynch, C. (2004) *Interoperability between Library Information Services and Learning Environments—Bridging the Gaps*. Lake Mary, FL: IMS Global Learning Consortium.

Minor, C. and Dunning, B. (2006) 'Making virtual library staffing a reality', *Information Outlook*, 10(5): 29–32.

Morgan, E. L. (2005) 'MyLibrary', available at *http://dewey.library.nd.edu/mylibrary* (accessed 28 September 2006).

Moyo, L. (2004) 'Electronic libraries and the emergence of new service paradigms', *Electronic Library*, 22: 220–30.

Nicholas, D. (2003) 'Digital information consumers, players and purchasers: Information seeking behaviour in the new digital interactive environment', *Aslib Proceedings*, 55(1/2): 23–31.

North Carolina State University Library (2002) 'LOBO tutorial', available at *http://www.lib.ncsu.edu/lobo2/lobo2.php* (accessed 28 September 2006).

OCLC (2002) 'How academic librarians can influence students' web-based information choices', OCLC White Paper on The Information Habits of College Students, available at *http://www5.oclc.org/downloads/community/informationhabits.pdf* (accessed 28 September 2006).

OCLC (2005) *Perceptions of Libraries and Information Resources*, Dublin, OH: OCLC.

Oliver, K. and Swain, R. (2006) 'Directories of institutional repositories: Research results and recommendations', paper presented at the International Federation of Library Associations conference, Seoul, August.

Patrizio, A. (2006) 'Taming the digital beast', *Campus Technology* (June): 41–46.

Portmann, C. and Roush, A. (2004) 'Assessing the effects of library instruction', *Journal of Academic Librarianship*, 30(6): 461–5.

Prytherch, R. (Comp.) (2000) *Harrod's Librarians' Glossary and Reference Book* (9th edn), Aldershot: Gower.

Rainie, L. (2006) 'Life online: Teens and technology and the world to come', available at *http://www.pewInternet.org/presentation_archive.org* (accessed 10 April 2006).

Reference and User Services Association Access to Information Committee Information Services for Information Consumers (2000) 'Guidelines for Providers', available at *http://www.ala.org/ala/rusa/rusaprotools/referenceguide/guidelinesinformation.htm* (accessed 28 September 2006).

Rettig, J. (2004) 'Technology, cluelessness, anthropology and the memex: The future of academic reference service', Chicago: American Library Association, available at *http://www.ala.org/ala/rusa/rusaprotools/futureofref/technologycluelessness.htm* (accessed 28

September 2006).

Sarkodie-Mensah, K. (ed.) (2000) *Reference Services for the Adult Learner: Challenging Issues for the Traditional and Technological Era*, New York: Haworth Press.

Savolainen, R. (2006) 'Spatial factors as contextual qualifiers of information seeking', *Information Research*, 11(4): paper 261.

Sax, L. J (2003) 'Our incoming students: What are they like?', *About Campus*, 8(3): 15–20.

Sheth, J. (2002) 'Brand aid: Creating a presence in your community', paper presented at the American Library Association conference, Atlanta, June.

United Nations Educational, Scientific and Cultural Organization Bangkok. (2006). 'Performance indicators on ICT for education matrix', available at *http://www.unescobkk.org/index.php?id=1083* (accessed 10 April 2006).

University of California, Los Angeles, Library (2006) 'College library', available at *http://www.library.ucla.edu/libraries/college/* (accessed 29 September 2006).

University of Glasgow Humanities Advanced Technology and Information Institute and The National Initiative for a Networked Cultural Heritage (2002) 'NINCH guide to good practice in the digital representation and management of cultural heritage materials', available at *http://www.nyu.edu/its/humanities/ninchguide/index.html* (accessed 25 September 2006).

University of Illinois Urbana-Champaign Library (2006) 'I-Go library toolbar', available at *http://www.library.uiuc.edu/toolbar/* (accessed 28 September 2006).

Van de Sompel, H. and Hochstenbach, P. (1999) 'Reference linking in a hybrid library environment', *D-Lib*, 5(4), available at *http://www.dlib.org/dlib/april99/van_de_sompel/04van_de_sompel-pt1.html* (accessed 1 December 2006).

Walter, V. and Mediavilla, C. (2005) 'Teens are from Neptune, librarians are from Pluto: An analysis of online reference transactions', *Library Trends*, 54: 209–27.

Weise, F. (2004) 'Being there: the library as place', *Journal of the Medical Library Association*, 92(1): 6–13.

Wheatley, P (2004) *Institutional Repositories within the Context of Digital Preservation*. York: Digital Preservation Coalition.

Whitlatch, J. (2000) *Evaluating Reference Services: A Practical Guide*, Chicago: American Library Association.

Whitmire, E. (2001) 'The relationship between undergraduates' background characteristics and college experiences and their academic library use', *College and Research Libraries*, 62(6): 528–540.

Winter, K. (2000) 'From wood pulp to the web: the online evolution', *American Libraries*, 31(5): 70–74.

Young, A. (1983) *The ALA Glossary of Library and Information Science*, Chicago: American Library Association.

Index

academic community, xi–xii, 9–17, 28, 51–2, 54, 56, 60–3, 69, 80–1, 92–3, 100–4
accreditation, 52
action research, 99, 107–8
administrators, 16, 67, 95, 101, 108–9
  see also librarians
Aires electronic reserve system, xiv
Allard, S., 65
American Library Association, 32, 62, 66, 100
American Medical Association, 29
Americans with Disabilities Act 1990, 9, 77
Ask.com, xvii
assessment, 60, 92, 95–6, 103–7
  see also evaluation
Association of College & Research Libraries, 66, 90
Astin, A., 100
Atton, C., 8
audio, 57–58, 68
audio-visual service, xvi
Australia, 40
authentification, xv, 46, 64
  see also security
authority control, 39, 58

automated systems, xv, 34, 46–7, 63
  see also integrated library systems

Bailey, Charles, 69
Baron, Naomi, 5
Bazillion, Richard, 83, 97
Bejune, M., 81
Beloit College, 2
bibliographies, xiv, 41, 50–1, 56, 69, 75, 109
  see also webliographies
Black studies, 90, 92
blogs, xvii, 63, 86
Bloom, B., 92–3
Bordonaro, K., 94
Borek, D., 80
Borgman, C., 5
Boss, R., 78–9
Bradford, J., 87
Braun, C., 83, 97
Breivik, P., 104
Budapest Open Access Initiative, 69
Burke, G., 86
Bryne, A., 70

Caledonian University, 90–1
California Library Association, 25